"My American Dream"

Thomas R Meinders

iUniverse, Inc.
Bloomington

"My American Dream"

iUniverse books may be ordered through booksellers or by contacting:

iUniverse
1663 Liberty Drive
Bloomington, IN 47403
www.iuniverse.com
1-800-Authors (1-800-288-4677)

ISBN: 978-1-4502-7939-0 (sc)
ISBN: 978-1-4502-7940-6 (dj)
ISBN: 978-1-4502-7941-3 (ebook)

Printed in the United States of America

iUniverse rev. date: 12/28/2010

INTRODUCTION

"My American Dream" is the fourth in the series about the problems confronting the United States of America. The other members of the series are "Bashing Sarah Palin", "America Can Recover" and "A Beautiful America". These books will make some people smile, some Laugh, some will agree, some will disagree, some might cry and some will think I am crazy. The purpose is to make people think about what is happening in our government.

It doesn't matter whether you are a Democrat or Republican; make sure that your candidate is looking out for the people of your district. Remember it should be "We the People, By the People and For the People" and if your Representatives do not understand that then don't vote for them. Your vote really does matter.

It doesn't matter which side of the isle you vote on. Both sides play these games. Right now our political system is broken and I hope they keep on fighting so that more voting Americans will wake up, get involved and really take a good long look at both candidates no matter what letter is next to their names. Hopefully then we can get a few quality people back in Washington who actually vote what their districts really want. Politics is about open ideas and cooperation anyway. Isn't it?

Remember, there are only 545 people making decisions that affect the 307,745,000 American citizens. They are our President, the members of Congress, the members of the House of Representatives and the Supreme

Court. We need to make sure that these 545 people understand that they are responsible for making the decisions that protect the welfare of every American citizen. These people determine what the federal budget will be. If they want a deficit, the United States will have a deficit. Hold every representative to the responsibility of creating a balanced budget. When the government wants to solve the illegal migrant problem they have the resources but they need to decide they want to. The stimulus programs were devised by these individuals and did not take into consideration what the citizens wanted. If these 545 representatives that are supposed to be taking care of America would have done their jobs and consulted the American citizen there would not have been 787 billion dollars wasted on the stimulus program. The healthcare fiasco would not have happened if they would have listened to the citizens. Instead, they chose to follow the leader and give in to President Obama. The Constitution which is the supreme law of the land, gives sole responsibility to the House of Representatives for originating and approving appropriations and taxes. The speaker of the House and fellow members, not the President, can approve any budget they want. If the President vetoes it, they can pass it over his veto if they agree to. We need to balance the budget.

GOD BLESS AMERICA

TABLE OF CONTENTS

CHAPTER ONE:

My American Dream

My dream for America would be to return the country to the core values that our funding fathers had in mind when they wrote the "Declaration of Independence" and the United States "Constitution".

America needs to return the language of our country to English. Until the country starts to enforce the policies that are in the requirements for citizenship we are going to continue to have groups of illegals that think they have special rights and do not need to learn the customs of the United States and to speak our language which is English.

I would like to see the return of God in our federal government. There needs to be an education of our youth in the schools about our country. The Pledge of Allegiance needs to be said in school each morning with the students understanding that they face the flag with their hands on their hearts. In an assembly or athletic event for the school the playing of the National Anthem would be required with the student body singing along. This would teach every student some of the core values of being American. All schools will only instruct the students in English.

America is in desperate need of a President that thinks it proper to spend time in the Oval Office of the White House to actually conduct some business for the United States. It appears that the President is already getting ready to start campaigning for the elections of 2012. Obama has requested for every possible record of the nine most likely Republican candidates that might be running in 2012. Sure looks like Obama is looking for all the things the Republicans could have done in high school or kindergarten to start the dirty political campaign like they did for the mid-terms elections of 2010. My American Dream would be for every politician to run a campaign on what they are going to do for the citizens of the United States. I mean all the citizens and not just the ones that might vote for them. The President needs to spend more time in the Oval office and less time out campaigning.

Why are the federal courts interfering with what the citizens want regarding illegals? Arizona voter citizen proof requirement overturned. The federal government and their Democratic appointed judges are at it again.

A federal appeals court struck down an Arizona requirement that residents prove United States citizenship in order to register to vote but upheld a mandate that they present identification before casting their ballots. What is the matter with this judge?

Opponents of the 6-year-old law incorporating both provisions -- designed to prevent illegal immigrants from voting -- said the ruling would likely lead to thousands being turned away from the mid-term elections. They should be turned away if they do not have the proper proof that they are American citizens and do not know how to read a ballot that should only be printed in the language of the United States which is English. Good for Arizona.

The state denied registration of an estimated 30,000 Arizonans who failed to prove their citizenship during the first four years of the law, said John Greenbaum, legal director for the Lawyers' Committee for Civil Rights under Law, one of the groups challenging the statute. This idiot attorney needs to get his head out of the desert sands of Arizona. His organization hailed Tuesday's decision to strike down the proof of citizenship requirement as "a great victory for voting rights advocates." What about the rights of the real citizens of the United States that do not want illegals having a method of voting? These people are illegals and they do not have any rights since they are criminals.

A joint statement by Arizona Governor Jan Brewer and Secretary of State Ken Bennett, both Republicans, called the ruling "an outrage and a slap in the face to all Arizonans who care about the integrity of their elections."

The ruling stems from a ballot initiative, Proposition 200, Arizona voters passed in 2004 requiring individuals to produce proof of citizenship, such as a passport, to register to vote, and a picture ID, such as a driver's license, or two pieces of non-photo ID, in order to cast a ballot.

Proposition 200 opponents have argued the polling ID requirements discriminate against minorities and the poor, who might not have the money to obtain the necessary proof of identification. If they can't prove they are legal citizens then they should be sent back where they came from not given rights to vote.

When the federal government provides citizenship verification to its residents, makes it mandatory to present said verification before receiving any city, state or federal services or licenses: and enforces laws making it a felony with mandatory jail time for misrepresenting citizenship status, then we can address illegal invader activity. This will apply to every person within our borders regardless of ethnicity, thereby eliminating any possibility of profiling on any level. It would serve all socio-economic levels we have equally and prevent all voter fraud. This would also serve as a way to effectively provide social services across the board. Could it be abused? Everything can be abused. We are being abused the way things are by criminals who have no qualms about flaunting their illegality in our faces now.

The advocacy groups say this decision to strike down the proof of citizenship requirement as "a great victory for voting rights advocates." Translation: means more illegal voters to vote Democratic to get government freebies and expand the federal hold on legal citizens.

Directly from the Federal Mail in Registration Form: how to find out if you are eligible to register to vote in your State. Each State has its own laws about who may register and vote. Check the information under your State in the State Instructions. All States require that you be a United States citizen by birth or naturalization to register to vote in federal and State elections. Federal law makes it illegal to falsely claim United States citizenship to register to vote in any federal, State, or local election. You cannot be registered to vote in more than one place at a time.

This is why a National United States ID card is needed (with picture and PIN number). To identify you are that person. To get a job, rent or buy a home, send your kids to school, get a driver's license, obtain the vast array of social programs (when needed), obtain credit and where you resided. By cutting off everything for illegals, they have no choice but to go home. No more: housing, food stamps, education, jobs, utilities, public services, etc. They will self-deport! Zero cost to the tax payer. This alone will close California's budget gap.

The National United States ID card will be needed for voting. No more dead people coming out of the grave to vote. No more vote early and often. No more illegal alien voting. No more voting fraud. If you're here illegally you have no rights as a United States citizen. Go home.

I agree we should all have to prove our citizenship when registering to vote. When one first gets their drivers license they have show a birth certificate, which should prove citizenship. A citizen should also have a different type of driver's license than a non citizen, so when applying for their driver's license renewal they can also register to vote.

There is good news from Arizona. The latest figures show that over 100,000 illegals have left the state since the SB-1070 law was passed earlier this year. The study worked with figures from the United States Current Population Survey. The study says the decline could be due to the law known as SB1070, which partly entered into effect in July, or to Arizona's difficult economic situation. The study also cites Mexican government figures as saying that 23,380 Mexicans returned from Arizona to Mexico between June and September of 2010. That is a start but the United States census figures from 2008 indicate that there were 1.9 million Hispanics living in Arizona.

Arizona is in the process of appealing a ruling that put on hold parts of the SB-1070 law, which would have allowed police to question the immigration status of those they suspect are in the country illegally.

Immigrants are heavily employed in Arizona's construction industry, which has suffered along with the rest of the state's economy in the economic downturn. This sure contradicts the theory that the only jobs the illegals do are picking strawberries, watermelons and tomatoes.

Further studies predict that the amount of money that is sent back to Mexico by illegals working in the United States is estimated at $26 billion annually. The remittances are Mexico's second largest source of income after oil exports. This money comes from the 20,000,000 million illegals that are living in the United States.

If I were to run for the Office of President of the United States I would make the following information my platform and run on the party of common sense. My qualifications are that I am an American and proud of it and can prove it. I have served my country in the United States Air Force. I have a Masters degree from the school of hard knocks and survived. My platform is as follows:

- ◉ Why does everyone believe it's the government's job to create jobs? It's not. Real jobs and a robust economy are created by the enterprise of private sector companies. The government only creates jobs that are funded by tax funds and they do not create revenue. Most government entities are very poorly managed and lose billions every year.

- ◉ Close the USPS. It's losing billions every year. Turn it over to the private sector.

- ◉ Make everyone who has been living on welfare work for some level of government to earn the welfare check.

- ◉ Secure our borders and deport all illegals out of the United States. Support legal immigration.

- ◉ Construct a secure barrier between United States and Mexico.

- ◉ Require Fannie Mae and Freddie Mac to become private entities. Get the government out of the mortgage business.

◉ Remove all unions from government entities. Why would government workers need a union? Is our government a bad employer?

◉ Immediately remove unions from the public education system.

◉ Repeal the Cap and Trade Bill (American Clean Energy and Security Tax H.R. 2454). The bill established a "Cap-and-Trade" regime to reduce carbon emissions to slow "global warming." Also known as "Cap-and-Tax," the bill would impose a new national energy tax costing each American family about $3,000 per year on average. It is estimated to increase unemployment by 1,105,000 jobs per year.

◉ Repeal Obamacare Private Health Care Takeover (Affordable Healthcare for America Act H.R. 3962) This Obamacare bill slashed Medicare benefits by nearly $500 billion for Seniors who paid into the system their entire working lives, while increasing taxes $565 billion. The bill requires private insurers to add applicants with pre-existing conditions and children to the age of 26, raising private health insurance costs for most working Americans and small business. Bill mandates that 30 million Americans buy private insurance or receive free government care. Bill provides for "rationing" for life-saving medical procedures. The Congressional Budget Office estimates Obamacare will add $1 trillion to federal costs over the next decade.

◉ Remove the government from of all private sector businesses.

◉ Pass term limit legislation for Congress, Senators and the Supreme Court.

◉ Immediately begin drilling for oil and natural gas in the United States.

This item is from pages 43 and 44 of the President's proposed federal budget for the year ending September 30, 2011.

Opening Government Up to the American People

The President has been clear from day one in office: the Federal Government must break down the barriers between it and the people it is supposed to serve. Through an unprecedented Open Government Directive, he put transparency, participation, and collaboration at the center of the Government's operations. In response, every Cabinet agency, along with the White House, has taken a range of steps to open government up to the American people. These include the release of information, such as the White House visitor logs; efforts to get citizen input and comment on executive orders; and the use of online technologies so the public can ask questions of their Government leaders. In addition, the Administration has moved affirmatively to reduce special interest influence on the Federal Government through, for example, restrictions on lobbying related to the Recovery Act and financial stabilization efforts and a ban on lobbyists serving on agency advisory boards and commissions, bodies which had become dominated by special interests. Transparency not only strengthens the bond between citizens and their Government, it also boosts performance by strengthening accountability, supporting the identification of effective practices, stimulating idea flow, and motivating better performance. Online posting of performance data—including agency goals, performance trends, improper payments and IT projects—represents an important step toward creating a culture of accountability in government. Openness also can improve the quality of the services delivered to citizens. Transparent processes allow citizens to offer feedback on service quality to make government better, improving satisfaction levels. To further open up the government to the American People.

How many American's have really seen anything that remotely resembles the above statements that are contained in the budget? The government has done more to become secretive about what they are going to pass legislation on then at any time in the history of the United States. There is no transparency whatsoever. It is designed to sound like the President is actually trying to do something positive instead of his real life back door political maneuvers.

Make It Easier to Track How Taxpayer Dollars Are Spent.

For too long, Americans have been in the dark about how their tax dollars are spent. They pay their taxes, but have no clear, concise way to track how and where the money is spent and what it accomplishes. The Administration is committed to pulling back the curtain on Government spending and will launch a new tracking tool with daily updates that will provide citizens with the ability to see aggregate spending by agency and also by geographic area. A new search engine will allow the public to customize their information by location, by agency, or by timeframe. This innovative development will allow people to have a greater understanding of how their Government works, and hold officials accountable for responsible spending decisions.

Has anyone seen how they spent the $800 billion stimulus package? How about an accounting of all the other pieces of legislation that have cost the taxpayers billions of dollars?

CHAPTER TWO:

Smaller Government

The United States needs to reduce the size of the federal government. We can accomplish this by eliminating many of the departments that have very little or no useful purpose in our current society. These departments have become drags on the economy and have out lived the purpose that they were established for.

When the government implements the policy of reducing every government employee's salary by 25% there will be enough attrition from the unhappy employees that will reduce the number of employees and payroll at the same time.

Fannie Mae and Freddie Mac should be forced out of the mortgage guarantee program and let the lending institutes be responsible for making loans on the merits of the home buyers credit rating, earnings record, proper down payment and availability of emergency funds. As hard as it is there is just not any reason to believe that every American should be able to own a home. The practice of lending to unqualified buyers has been the major contributing factor to the mortgage crises. The government does not know how to run any business not alone guaranteeing mortgages that they have no idea who are the homeowners.

The federal government could eliminate 20% of the employees on the payroll and the efficiency of the government would probably improve. The remaining workers would understand that they must produce at certain levels or they will be the next ones that are given pink slips. There should not be any unions involved with the government employees. The unions are not interested in the welfare and interests of the American citizens.

The government needs to eliminate the Department of Education and return all educational policies back to the state and local level. The government does not have any idea about running a school system. Each local school district has its own set of problems and can't be solved by a blanket directive from the federal government. This would eliminate a huge bureaucratic department and the schools would be able to educate in the proper manner. The states should make it a requirement that there will be no child held back instead of no child left behind. If the student can't keep up they should be held back a year. The states should all pass legislation that the only language in the school systems will be English. If a student does not know how to speak and write English they need to be put into a special English class until they can perform up to the level of the Americans in the school. This will not set well with most of the teachers but the unions should be abolished from all educational programs. If the teachers want a raise then produce exceptional results. Another benefit would be that if the teachers do not get a raise they will not be able to strike and the students unable to attend school.

The student loan division of the Department of Education would be transferred to the banking industry. There are way too many student loans that have not been repaid and the government will probably never see these loans paid.

On page 37 of the Presidents proposed budget for the year ending September 30, 2011 he states that the government is laying a new foundation for economic growth and prosperity for working families will take a change in policies and programs to unleash the creativity and hard work of the American people. But to prevent our country from backsliding into the irresponsibility of the past, we need to change how Washington works. We have seen the consequences of fiscal recklessness, of tolerance for programs that no longer work or are outdated, and of a government that is most open to those with access and influence. The deficits, wasted resources, and special treatment squandered funds that could have been used to help Americans gain or retain a foothold in the middle class and enjoy what every family wants: a good job, a roof over their heads, excellent schools for their children, affordable and high-quality health care, and a secure retirement.

Wow! The President must be smoking some really powerful cigarettes. The President's writers are completely out of touch with what has happened to America since Obama became the President. Has anyone noticed anything in this rhetoric that has actually happened? The next paragraph is also from the budget and guess where the blame is going to be placed?

Restoring Fiscal Discipline

When the President took office he faced a deficit of $1.3 trillion for that first fiscal year, a far cry from the budget surpluses predicted at the start of the previous administration. Since the 2010 Budget was released in February of 2009, unfavorable economic conditions and technical re-estimates have worsened the deficit outlook by $2 trillion through 2019—the equivalent of 1 percent of GDP per year—with a deterioration of about $200 billion in 2015 alone. Looking out over the next decade, we are $12 trillion deeper in debt than we were in 2001 because of three specific developments. The national debt is $7.5 trillion larger by the end of this decade because of the failure to pay for two large tax cuts, primarily for the wealthiest Americans, and a new entitlement program. An additional $3 trillion in debt is the result of inheriting the worst recession since the Great Depression. Our response to this recession, the Recovery Act, which has been critical to restoring economic growth, added an additional $1 trillion to the debt— only 10 percent of the total. Now, as we turn the corner from rescuing the economy to rebuilding it, it's time to once again take responsibility for our fiscal future. While it's essential that we do not stifle the momentum of our recovery from the current recession, we also cannot adequately grow the economy and spur job creation in the long term if we allow these deficits to persist. That is why, as the economy recovers, the Administration will take the steps necessary to restore discipline to our Nation's finances to put our country on firm fiscal footing.

The President sure knows how to spread the donkey dung. In what part of the United States has this recovery started? The recovery has started only in the minds of the Democrats and their lemming economists. The American people sure have not seen any real signs of recovery. The rhetoric above does not agree with the numbers that most of the country is seeing. The deficit at the end of the budget year discussed will be more like $13.5 to $14 trillion. The President has instigated policies that have increased the budget more in two years that the rest of the Presidents of the United States combined.

CHAPTER THREE:

Lower Income Tax Rates

The government needs to keep the income tax rates at the levels of the Bush tax cuts for everyone. Wasn't it part of the President's campaigning that if he was elected the government would not raise taxes?

How about page 39 of the President's budget proposal for the year ending in 2011?

Allow the Bush Tax Cuts for Households Earning More Than $250,000 to Expire.

In the last Administration, those at the very top enjoyed large tax breaks and income gains while almost everyone else struggled and real income for the middle class declined. Our Nation cannot afford to continue these tax cuts, which is why the President supports allowing those tax cuts that affect families earning more than $250,000 a year to expire and committing these resources to reducing the deficit instead. This step will have no effect on the 98 percent of all households who make less than $250,000 per year.

Reduce the Itemized Deduction Write-off for Families with Incomes over $250,000.

Currently, if a middle-class family donates a dollar to its favorite charity or spends a dollar on mortgage interest, it gets a 15-cent tax deduction, but a millionaire who does the same enjoys a deduction that is more than twice as generous. By reducing this disparity and returning the high income deduction to the same rates that were in place at the end of the Reagan Administration, we will raise $291 billion over the next decade.

This type of propaganda is unrealistic. The President does not know what is going to happen next year not alone the next decade. It is nothing more than a feeble attempt to ease public opinion and is not based on any facts. The President continues to exaggerate the effects of his proposed policies to try and gain political support. The American people are not buying into the rhetoric any more.

Then we have the President proposing that we eliminate funding for inefficient fossil fuel subsidies. What the President should be doing instead of eliminating incentives for development of fossil fuel is creating better programs to promote the development of the fossil fuels that are abundantly available in the United States and eliminate most of the annual trade deficit.

Eliminate Funding for Inefficient Fossil Fuel Subsidies.

As we work to create a clean energy economy, it is counter productive to spend taxpayer dollars on incentives that run counter to this national priority. To further this goal and reduce the deficit, the Budget eliminates tax preferences and funding for programs that provide inefficient fossil fuel subsidies that impede investment in clean energy sources and undermine efforts to deal with the threat of climate change. We are eliminating 12 tax breaks for oil, gas, and coal companies, closing loopholes to raise nearly $39 billion over the next decade.

Here we go again with what is gong to happen in the next decade. At the current rate of spending by this President we will be so far in debt our children and grand children will never be able to repay

the countries debt. Instead of looking at ways to cut the deficit he is looking at ways to discourage the exploration of our abundant assets that are available that could eliminate the deficit. It just doesn't make any sense.

Recommit to Cutting the Deficit in Half by the End of the President's First Term.

Even though he entered office facing an historic economic and financial crisis, the President committed his Administration to cutting the deficit he inherited upon taking office in half by the end of his first term. Since then, it has become clear that the recession was worse than anyone thought at the beginning of 2009, costing the Government even more in assistance and lost revenue. Nonetheless, the President remains committed to cutting in half by the end of his first term the deficit he inherited on January 20, 2009.

The President must be under the belief that taxpayers will not read any part of the proposed budget for the year 2011. How can he possible by so incompetent to believe that the taxpayers will not see through these outright lies? The current administration has not cut the deficit after his first full in office where he was responsible but has added $1.2 billion to the deficit and the 2011 budget proposals is going to add another $1.29 billion. That is really cutting the deficit in half. Why does the President keep lying to the people that he is supposed to be representing? It is just not the American way. If you would like a PDF copy of the budget send an email to: meinders@aol.com

We actually have a civil war going on in this country between the liberal extremists, led by Obama and his cohorts and staffed with foot soldiers from the public service unions, against the rest of Americans. These people want more and more tax money that they can distribute to their friends who keep them in power, they want bigger government and government control so that they can stay in power, they want to control private companies

Does anyone remember that Obama had promised not to raise taxes on the citizens of the United States? There is legislation to impose a 1% transaction tax on everyone in America. The bill is HR-4646 and was introduced by Representative Peter DeFazio (D-OR) and Senator Tom Harkin (D-IA). The bill is in committee and will probably not be brought out for vote until after the mid-term elections. The 1% transaction tax is proposed by President Obama's finance team and their plan is to sneak it in after the elections to keep it under the radar. This is a 1% tax on all transactions at any financial institution. That means all transactions including deposits at your bank, purchase of stocks, withdrawals from your bank and all transactions. This is from the President that promised that if you make under $250,000 per year you will not see one penny of new tax. Keep your eyes and ears open and you will be amazed at what you learn about our current administration. Well some will say it is only 1%. Just remember that once a tax is in place the rate can easily be raised.

One percent transaction tax is proposed by President Obama's finance team is recommending a transaction tax. His plan is to sneak it in after the November election to keep it under the radar. This is a 1% tax on all transactions at any financial institution including the banks, credit unions, etc. Any deposit you make, or move around within your account will have a 1% tax charged. If your pay check or your social security or whatever is direct deposit this 1% tax will be charged. If you hand carry a check in to deposit, 1% tax charged, if you take cash in to deposit, and 1% tax charged. The bill would tax 58 million seniors more than the annual amount of money that they were hoping to receive in their annual increases in social security. If a senior citizen receives $1,200 per month this 1% tax will cost the senior $24.00 per month which will be more than the average increase they would normally receive. Not to mention that the seniors will not receive any increase again in 2011.

Some will say aw it's just 1%... remember once the tax is there they can raise it at will.

Pelosi: Transaction Tax Has "Great Deal of Merit"

A proposed tax on financial transactions "has a great deal of merit" and would help Congress raise needed revenue, U.S. House of Representatives Speaker Nancy Pelosi said.

"I believe that the transaction tax still has a great deal of merit," Pelosi said at a news conference.

The tax would have a "really minimal impact on the transaction, but a tremendous impact on helping us meet our needs," Pelosi said.

Now that you have seen what the Pelosi has said about this tax why don't we look at the bill that the Democrats are trying to shove down our throats?

The bill is HR-4646 introduced by US Rep Peter DeFazio D-Oregon and US Senator Tom Harkin D-Iowa. It is now in committee and will probably not be brought out until after the Nov. elections. Suggest that you pass this along and also to your state senator and representative and US Congressman and Senators.

H.R. 4646

The bill proposed a One percent transaction tax. You can go to into THOMAS (Library of Congress and print out and read the entire bill. It contains 15 pages. The bill has been given the short title of "Debt Free America Act." It is the most socialistic bill that could ever been proposed. It needs to be stopped.

Just think, if you deposit $5,000.00 into your checking account or savings account the bank has to take out 1% or $50.00 of that money and send it to Washington. Then, any checks or cash you take out of your bank they will deduct 1% from what is still in the bank and send it to Washington. Total put in the Bank $5,000.00. $100.00 of that you give to Washington. Isn't this triple + Taxation?

This bill, spells it out that everyone will pay the Government 1% of their gross income.

Page 9 states the House and Senate shall convene not later than November 23, 2010 and Page 11 states the vote on passage shall occur not later than December 23, 2010.

CHAPTER FOUR:

Eliminating Pork Projects

The Congress needs to pass legislation that bans all pork attachments to any piece of legislation that is proposed in both houses. Every bill that is presented should be able to stand on the merits of the legislation. If it can't be passed without bribing the members with pork the bill probably was not for the benefit of the people of the United States.

The Citizens Against Government Waste puts out an annual "Congressional Pig Book" that listed 9,129 projects at a cost of $16.5 billion in 2010.

I would like to see a total breakdown of the $800 billion stimulus bill to include each and every project that was in the bill. How many pork projects were attached to the bill to get it passed. The government needs to provide a complete accounting for each project that was funded by the bill. That includes engineering cost, labor cost, material cost and all other expenses. When the accounting is received it could reveal just how many jobs were created for non union members that were not employed by the contractors who received the project money. How many jobs did this massive spending bill create for the unemployed?

The Obama administration needs to make a full disclosure about the healthcare legislation. The citizens of the United States have the God given right to know what pork projects were attached to this bill. We already know that the requirement to have businesses prepare Form 1099's on every business that they sell or buy over $600 from. What other garbage attachments are on the healthcare bill? All of the pork attachments need to be repealed immediately.

Harry Reid the leader of the Senate started his campaigning in Nevada by bragging about his ability to bring hundreds of millions of dollars in federal pork back to the state of Nevada.

The Congress has created a federal government that's too big and too expensive. Every political candidate should swear off the earmarks. Congress needs to know that many of the systems or manifestations of the pork spending, which is the political lubricant that keeps this big machine going and keeps it growing. We need to decrease the size of government and not provide methods of making the government larger. Eliminate all pork spending.

Earmarks that were attached to the legislative bills in 2010 amounted to about $16.5 billion. The government has attached bring home the bacon attachments that the taxpayer's did not know anything about. If these attachments were so good they could have been stand alone bills and the whole Congress could have voted on them. That would be the transparent way of passing legislation.

The Democrats would have been in trouble if it were not for the pork earmarks. Without them the healthcare bill would not have been passed. It is the result of the bribes made to the Democrats that voted to pass the legislation. Every American should be contacting their representatives and demanding an accounting of what bacon went to each state. It is bad enough that there is not any transparency but to add to the insult there is not any accountability.

The following is an example of how the bringing home the bacon works. That's good. Whatever anyone thinks about Harry Reid or the Tea Party bragging about how much pork you've brought to a state is not a good thing.

A residence of Connecticut where they have the Coast Guard Academy and the Electric Boat Company that makes submarines for the Navy.

Every year, their two senators would brag about how much money they had procured for the Electric Boat Company to build submarines but the catch was THAT THE NAVY DIDN'T WANT THEM. So in essence, they spent billions building submarines that the United States Navy didn't want or need. That is not very good for all the taxpayers. I'm all for having a few extra jobs but not at the expense of the national economy. Polls rail against discretionary spending but defense spending is the largest portion of discretionary spending in the federal budget. It is just a jobs program and corporate welfare for defense contractors. Another reason the federal government should eliminate all the pork programs. This would not have passed as a stand alone piece of legislation.

Could it be that the pork problem is going to be heard? The anti-earmark candidates promise to shake up a Capitol culture in which earmarking is seen by most lawmakers as a birthright. In the House, Minority Leader John Boehner, R-Ohio, who has never sought an earmark, earlier this year orchestrated a Republican rules change in which the party swore off earmarks. Now they need to pass legislation that makes it illegal to have earmarks.

But renegades like Senators. Jim DeMint, (R-SC), and Tom Coburn, (R-OK) are pushing the party to give up earmarks. DeMint was counting on anti-earmark reinforcements from the election to help him force a vote on changing Republican conference rules to require Republicans to abandon the practice. An overwhelming majority of new Republican candidates have taken the no-pork pledge.

President Obama and all Incumbents your worst nightmare is going to happen. It is the American people waking up. Don't be afraid be very, very afraid, and we know you are, because we can tell by the desperation in the Democratic campaigns and all the fear that you are trying to place in the American voters minds. It is as palpable as the grass roots movement that is picking up speed and sweeping the nation. "We the People" may not be able to dislodge you all from your positions on Pork Hill, but a substantial number of you are about to be evicted and the remaining ones had better pass legislation that is for the people and not for the benefit of some representative's home district. We are your employers and you are the employees. You are supposed to be serving the people and not your political interests. You should be afraid of us and not us afraid of you. These things you have forgotten, in the course of turning deaf ears to your countries needs and wants while you pursue only that which will benefit you and your state. We are tired of the lies, the stealing and the deception. We will reclaim our country and you can't stop us.

Pork/earmarks amounts to buying/selling a vote, an action that would put the common voter in prison. In congress it is an acceptable practice done on a daily basis. This practice of give me this and I'll vote yes on this bill that I'm actually against has got to stop.

All of these vote buying earmarks are a huge part of the problem. Ban all earmarks. If you can't get broad support for a piece of legislation without resorting to bribery, it is probably not a good piece of legislation to begin with. The people have had enough of the back door deals and bribery.

CHAPTER FIVE:

The Return of Manufacturing

The return of manufacturing to the United States is going to be the most important factor in stabilizing and improving the economy. The manufacturing sector is the bread and butter of the middle class of Americans.

It is not now, nor should it ever be the government's job to provide, pay for, stimulate financially or create jobs. The only way the Government should stimulate jobs should be with reduced or eliminated taxes that are caused during job creation such as investment tax credits for research and development, acquiring capital items for production and lowering barriers to employment.

When United States companies are able to fairly compete against each other they make some of the best products and services in the world. When China subsidizes its entire manufacturing sector and keeps its prices low by forcing its labor force to work for substandard wages then they should be penalized by tariffs to sell their goods here.

The President has included on page 19 of his proposed budget for the year 2011 that the economy has been rescued from disaster and is on the road to recovery. We are no longer facing the potential collapse of our financial system and the country has avoided the depression many feared just a year ago. Our economy is growing; our markets are returning to functionality; and some of the losses of the past year have been restored. These indicators may be heartening to economists, but they are cold comfort to the millions who are out of work, communities that have seen industries downsized and factories shuttered, and the cities and towns who are finding it hard to provide services to their residents.

There are 7 million fewer jobs today than when the recession began in December 2007. Our President sure has speech writers that have their heads in the clouds. Ask any American if we are out of the recession?

It certainly looks like we need to return manufacturing to the United States and create the necessary jobs to replace the 7 million that have been lost in the past few years. Since the budget proposal has been in effect has there been any effort to present a plan by the federal government that would return manufacturing to the United States? How about eliminating the NAFTA for starts?

The budget continues stating that in the short-term, it is critical that we take steps to jumpstart job creation so that the nascent economic recovery is one that lifts American workers and families. Looking to the future, we know that in the high-tech, interdependent economy of the 21st Century, two of the most precious resources for any nation are the know-how and creativity of its people. Basic research across the sciences leads to discoveries and technologies that create whole industries, thousands of businesses, and millions of jobs. From bio-technology to information technology, we have seen that happen in our own time. Yet this is not the moment to rest on our past accomplishments; we must support invention and innovation today so that our scientists, engineers, and entrepreneurs can grow these businesses of tomorrow.

Such beautiful rhetoric that the President is spreading. To bad that it is just smoke screens. How about the line that this is not the moment to rest on our past accomplishments? Just what accomplishments is the President referring to? Unemployment has gone from 4.6% when he took office to 9.6% and remained there for many months. That is not the kind of accomplishment the people of the United States are going to compliment.

Ford Motor Company has again taken the lead in returning jobs to this sector with their plans to improve and expand their plants in Michigan. This will result in the formation of 1,200 new full time jobs at a cost of approximately $850 million. This type project will not only provide the full time jobs but will also create thousands of part time jobs during the construction phase. The construction phase could take 2 to 3 years to complete.

The American people should be proud of Ford Motor Company. They were the only auto maker that did not take any of the government's bailout money and they have proven to the American public that running a business should not be dependent upon government support and politics. The American people have responded and have purchased there products and as a result they are very profitable and a huge success. That is the American way.

The Ford Motor Company released their earnings report for the third quarter and reported their sixth straight quarter of profits and their best quarter in the decade. Ford's exceptional results were accomplished because they built automobiles that the Americans wanted and their products were highly rated.

Ford has shown that a properly managed American company can survive and compete. It is a shame that more companies have not taken the same approach but instead took the easy way out and went off shore to earn quick profits while abandoning the United States worker. That is a start now lets bring back more of the jobs that are going being done in foreign countries.

Did anyone happen to catch that speech Harry Reid made about how he and the Democrats saved the auto-industry, particularly Ford Motors? It's funny because Ford didn't take any money (and didn't sell out to the messiah and his cronies).

So Ford is making money and doing well. But what about the two pawns who did sign a pact with Obama and the Democrats. Oh wait...not so good. Why? It's simple, they sold out and Ford didn't.

By the way, did Harry ever retract that statement that he made about them giving Ford bail out money? Nope.

Not to mention that all the shareholders of Chrysler and General Motors were left with nothing while the government and the unions gained total control of both companies. Only in America can the government be so stupid and forget about the citizens.

Ford has shown the world how it should be done. No bailout money brought in great management to reorganize and get rid of infighting and waste, and develop a real vision with innovative product development that stresses quality over quantity. Mulally and Booth deserve a national award. Everyone should buy Ford.

All Americans hope the management from Chrysler and General Motors learn a lesson from Ford. Build quality products that the buying public wants. Chrysler and General Motors have dumped your top heavy management, now roll your sleeves up and get more effective and you too can share in the wealth. But General Motors needs to quit bragging about repaying your loan, three quarters of the total was done with TARP money. You both have a long way to go but Ford has proven it can be done. Now get with the program because America needs the jobs.

They saw the writing on the wall. They knew that they had to get good in order to survive, and they did. Ford's done some amazing work in the last few years. The Fusion was a solid car when it came out and only got better with the recent re-design, the new Taurus is awesome and the new Focus that's going to be coming out shows a lot of promise, and of course the most recent generation of the Mustang was a vast improvement over recent generations of it, with a freshening due out next model year. Ford's recent success is well-deserved. They've put out some very good products in the last 6-7 years, and as long as they stay on top of their game, they'll continue to change the public perception about American cars. Go, Ford, go!

The automaker said it expects to end the year with as much cash as it has debt, a year earlier than it had previously forecast. Ford, which four years ago mortgaged its factories, blue oval logo and other assets to fund a huge restructuring, said it paid off $2 billion in debt in the third quarter and expects to pay off an additional $3.6 billion for retiree health care on Friday. Ford's debt will stand at $22.8 billion after those two actions. It has $20.3 billion in cash.

When Ford pays its debt to the United Auto Workers health care trust, it will no longer owe any money to the trust.

Ford previously said it plans to spend $950 million to revamp its Michigan Assembly plant to build a new version of the Focus compact car, due in dealer showrooms early next year. An electric-version of the Focus as well as next generation hybrid and plug-in hybrid vehicles are also all planned for production at the plant by 2012.

CHAPTER SIX:

The Loss of Manufacturing

Unfortunately the United States needs to address the companies that are moving the manufacturing jobs out of the United States. These companies should be hit with a tariff on all reported payroll that they ship out of the United States. When you make the cost of doing business in other countries comparable to the United States these companies will start thinking about America instead of increased corporate profits at the expense of the United States economy. Every one of these companies should be boycotted by the American citizens. When they lose their sales from being irresponsible to the needs of the country they will realize the mistakes they made. The only way is to make these companies pay for their lack of patriotism.

Here is a list of companies we've confirmed are "Exporting America." These are U.S. companies either sending American jobs overseas, or choosing to employ cheap overseas labor, instead of American workers. There are about 750 companies on this list that are not helping the United States and the unemployment problems. If each of these companies would bring back 200 of the jobs that they are filling overseas we would immediately create 150,000 jobs in the United States. Think about how many jobs would be created if they stopped sending jobs overseas. How about every American boycotting these companies by not purchasing their products or services?

Aalfs Manufacturing
Aavid Thermal Technologies
Access Electronics
Accuride Corporatio
ADC
Adobe Systems
Advanced Energy Industries
Aetna
Affiliated Computer Services
AFS Technologies
A.G. Edwards
Agere Systems
Agilent Technologies
AIG
Alamo Rent A Car
Albany International Corp.
Albertson's
Alcoa
Alcoa Fujikura
Allen Systems Group
Alliance Semiconductor
Allstate
Alpha Thought Global
Altria Group
Amazon.com
AMD
Americ Disc
American Dawn
American Express
American Greetings
American Household
American Management Systems
American Standard
American Uniform Company
AMETEK
AMI DODUCO
Amloid Corporation
Amphenol Corporation
Analog Devices

Anchor Glass Container
ANDA Networks
Anderson Electrical Products
Andrew Corporation
Anheuser-Busch
Angelica Corporation
Ansell Health Care
Ansell Protective Products
Anvil Knitwear
AOL
A.O. Smith
Apple
Applied Materials
Ark-Les Corporation
Arlee Home Fashions
Art Leather Manufacturing
Artex International
ArvinMeritor
Asco Power Technologies
Ashland
AstenJohnson
Asyst Technologies
Atchison Products, Inc.
A.T. Cross Company
AT&T
AT&T Wireless
A.T. Kearney
Augusta Sportswear
Authentic Fitness Corporation
Automatic Data Processing
Avanade
Avanex
Avaya
Avery Dennison
Azima Healthcare Services
Axiohm Transaction Solutions
ABC-NACO
Accenture
Accuride International

B
Bank of America
Bank of New York
Bank One
Bard Access Systems
Barnes Group
Barth & Dreyfuss of California
Bassett Furniture
Bassler Electric Company
BBi Enterprises L.P.
Beacon Blankets
BearingPoint
Bear Stearns
BEA Systems
Bechtel
Becton Dickinson
BellSouth
Bentley Systems
Berdon LLP
Berne Apparel
Bernhardt Furniture
Best Buy
Bestt Liebco Corporation
Beverly Enterprises
Birdair, Inc.
BISSELL
Black & Decker
Blauer Manufacturing
Blue Cast Denim
Bobs Candies
Borden Chemical
Bourns
Bose Corporation
Bowater
BMC Software
Boeing
Braden Manufacturing
Briggs Industries

Brady Corporation
Bristol-Myers Squibb
Bristol Tank & Welding Co.
Brocade
Brooks Automation
Brown Wooten Mills Inc.
Buck Forkardt, Inc.
Bumble Bee
Burle Industries
Burlington House Home Fashions
Burlington Northern and Santa Fe
Railway

C
Cadence Design Systems
Camfil Farr
Candle Corporation
Cains Pickles
Capital One
Cardinal Brands
Carrier
Carter's
Caterpillar
C-COR.net
C&D Technologies
Cellpoint Systems
Cendant
Centis, Inc.
Cerner Corporation
Charles Schwab
ChevronTexaco
The Cherry Corporation
CIBER
Ciena
Cigna
Circuit City
Cirrus Logic
Cisco Systems
Citigroup

Clear Pine Mouldings
Clorox
CNA
Coastcast Corp.
Coca-Cola
Cognizant Technology Solutions
Collins & Aikman
Collis, Inc.
Columbia House
Comcast Holdings
Comdial Corporation
Computer Associates
Computer Horizons
Computer Sciences Corporation
CompuServe
Concise Fabricators
Conectl Corporation
Conseco
Consolidated Metro
Continental Airlines
Convergys
Cooper Crouse-Hinds
Cooper Tire & Rubber
Cooper Tools
Cooper Wiring Devices
Copperweld
Cordis Corporation
Corning
Corning Cable Systems
Corning Frequency Control
Countrywide Financial
COVAD Communications
Covansys
Creo Americas
Cross Creek Apparel
Crouzet Corporation
Crown Holdings
CSX
Cummins

Cutler-Hammer
Cypress Semiconductor

D

Dana Corporation
Daniel Woodhead
Davis Wire Corp.
Daws Manufacturing
Dayton Superior
DeCrane Aircraft
Delco Remy
Dell Computer
DeLong Sportswear
Delphi
Delta Air Lines
Delta Apparel
Direct TV
Discover
DJ Orthopedics
Document Sciences Corporation
Dometic Corp.
Donaldson Company
Douglas Furniture of California
Dow Chemical
Dresser
Dun & Bradstreet
DuPont

E

Earthlink
Eastman Kodak
Eaton Corporation
Edco, Inc.
Editorial America
eFunds
Edscha
Ehlert Tool Company
Elbeco Inc.
Electroglas

Electronic Data Systems
Electronics for Imaging
Electro Technology
Eli Lilly
Elmer's Products
E-Loan
EMC
Emerson Electric
Emerson Power Transmission
Emglo Products
Engel Machinery
En Pointe Technologies
Equifax
Ernst & Young
Essilor of America
Ethan Allen
Evenflo
Evergreen Wholesale Florist
Evolving Systems
Evy of California
Expedia
Extrasport
ExxonMobil

F
Fairfield Manufacturing
Fair Isaac
Fansteel Inc.
Farley's & Sathers Candy Co.
Fasco Industries
Fawn Industries
Fayette Cotton Mill
FCI USA
Fedders Corporation
Federal Mogul
Federated Department Stores
Fellowes
Fender Musical Instruments
Fidelity Investments

Financial Techologies International
Findlay Industries
First American Title Insurance
First Data
First Index
Fisher Hamilton
Flowserve
Fluor
FMC Corporation
Fontaine International
Ford Motor
Foster Wheeler
Franklin Mint
Franklin Templeton
Freeborders
Frito Lay
Fruit of the Loom

G
Garan Manufacturing
Gateway
GE Capital
GE Medical Systems
Gemtron Corporation
General Binding Corporation
General Cable Corp.
General Electric
General Motors
Generation 2 Worldwide
Genesco
Georgia-Pacific
Gerber Childrenswear
GlobespanVirata
Goldman Sachs
Gold Toe Brands
Goodrich
Goodyear Tire & Rubber
Google
Graphic Controls

Greenpoint Mortgage
Greenwood Mills
Grote Industries
Grove U.S. LLC
Guardian Life Insurance
Guilford Mills
Gulfstream Aerospace Corp.

H
Haggar
Halliburton
Hamilton Beach/Procter-Silex
The Hartford Financial Services Group
Harper-Wyman Company
Hasbro Manufacturing Services
Hawk Corporation
Hawker Power Systems, Inc.
Haworth
Headstrong
HealthAxis
Hedstrom
Hein-Werner Corp.
Helen of Troy
Helsapenn Inc.
Hershey
Hewitt Associates
Hewlett-Packard
Hoffman Enclosures, Inc.
Hoffman/New Yorker
The Holmes Group
Home Depot
Honeywell
HSN
Hubbell Inc.
Humana
Hunter Sadler
Hutchinson Sealing Systems, Inc
HyperTech Solutions

I
IBM
iGate Corporation
Illinois Tool Works
IMI Cornelius
Imperial Home Decor Group
Indiana Knitwear Corp.
IndyMac Bancorp
Infogain
Ingersoll-Rand
Innodata Isogen
Innova Solutions
Insilco Technologies
Intel
InterMetro Industries
International Paper
Interroll Corporation
Intuit
Invacare
Iris Graphics, Inc.
Isola Laminate Systems
Iteris Holdings, Inc.
ITT Educational Services
ITT Industries

J
Jabil Circuit
Jacobs Engineering
Jacuzzi
Jakel, Inc.
JanSport
Jantzen Inc.
JDS Uniphase
Jockey International
John Crane
John Deere
Johns Manville
Johnson Controls

Johnson & Johnson
JPMorgan Chase
J.R. Simplot
Juniper Networks
Justin Brands

K
KANA Software
Kaiser Permanente
Kanbay
Kayby Mills of North Carolina
Keane
Kellogg
Kellwood
KEMET
KEMET Electronics
Kendall Healthcare
Kenexa
Kentucky Apparel
Kerr-McGee Chemical
KeyCorp
Key Industries
Key Safety Systems
Key Tronic Corp.
Kimberly-Clark
KLA-Tencor
Knight Textile Corp.
Kojo Worldwide Corporation
Kraft Foods
K2 Inc.
Kulicke and Soffa Industries
Kwikset

L
Lancer Partnership
Lander Company
LaCrosse Footwear
Lamb Technicon
Lau Industries

Lands' End
Lawson Software
Layne Christensen
Leach International
Lear Corporation
Leech Tool & Die Works
Lehman Brothers
Leoni Wiring Systems
Levi Strauss
Leviton Manufacturing Co.
Lexmark International
Lexstar Technologies
Liebert Corporation
Lifescan
Lillian Vernon
Linksys
Linq Industrial Fabrics, Inc.
Lionbridge Technologies
Lionel
Littelfuse
LiveBridge
LNP Engineering Plastics
Lockheed Martin
Longaberger
Louisiana-Pacific Corporation
Louisville Ladder Group LLC
Lowe's
Lucent
Lund International
Lyall Alabama

M
Madill Corporation
Magma Design Automation
Magnequench
Magnetek
Maidenform
Mallinckrodt, Inc.
The Manitowoc Company

Manugistics

Marathon Oil

Maritz

Mars

Marshall Fields

Mattel

Master Lock

Materials Processing, Inc.

Maxim Integrated Products

Maxi Switch

Maxxim Medical

Maytag

McDATA Corporation

McKinsey & Company

MeadWestvaco

Mediacopy

Medtronic

Mellon Bank

Mentor Graphics Corp.

Meridian Automotive Systems

Merit Abrasive Products

Merrill Corporation

Merrill Lynch

Metasolv

MetLife

Micro Motion, Inc.

Microsoft

Midcom Inc.

Midwest Electric Products

Milacron

Modern Plastics Technics

Modine Manufacturing

Moen

Money's Foods Us Inc.

Monona Wire Corp.

Monsanto

Morgan Stanley

Motion Control Industries

Motor Coach Industries International

Motorola

Mrs. Allison's Cookie Co.

Mulox

N

Nabco

Nabisco

NACCO Industries

National City Corporation

National Electric Carbon Products

National Life

National Semiconductor

NCR Corporation

neoIT

NETGEAR

Network Associates

Newell Rubbermaid

Newell Window Furnishings

New World Pasta

New York Life Insurance

Nice Ball Bearings

Nike

Nordstrom

Northrop Grumman

Northwest Airlines

Nu Gro Technologies

Nu-kote International

NutraMax Products

Nypro Alabama

O

O'Bryan Brothers Inc.

Ocwen Financial

Office Depot

Ogden Manufacturing

Oglevee, Ltd

Ohio Art

Ohmite Manufacturing Co.

Old Forge Lamp & Shade

Omniglow Corporation
ON Semiconductor
Orbitz
Oracle
OshKosh B'Gosh
Otis Elevator
Outsource Partners International
Owens-Brigam Medical Co.
Owens Corning
Oxford Automotive
Oxford Industries

P

Pacific Precision Metals
Pak-Mor Manufacturing
palmOne
Parallax Power Components
Paramount Apparel
Parker-Hannifin
Parsons E&C
Paxar Corporation
Pearson Digital Learning
Peavey Electronics CorporationÊÊ
PeopleSoft
PepsiCo
Pericom Semiconductor
PerkinElmer
PerkinElmer Life Sciences, Inc.
Perot Systems
Pfaltzgraff
Pfizer
Phillips-Van Heusen
Pinnacle West Capital Corporation
Pitney Bowes
Plaid Clothing Company
Planar Systems
Plexus
Pliant Corporation
PL Industries

Polaroid
Polymer Sealing Solutions
Portal Software
Portex, Inc.
Portola Packaging
Port Townsend Paper Corp.
Power One
Pratt & Whitney
Price Pfister
priceline.com
Pridecraft Enterprises
Prime Tanning
Primus Telecom
Procter & Gamble
Progress Lighting
ProQuest
Providian Financial
Prudential Insurance

Q

Quaker Oats
Quadion Corporation
Quantegy
Quark
Qwest Communications

R

Radio Flyer
Radio Shack
Rainbow Technologies
Rawlings Sporting Goods
Rayovac
Raytheon Aircraft
RCG Information Technology
Red Kap
Regal-Beloit Corporation
Regal Rugs
Respiratory Support Products
Regence Group

R.G. Barry Corp.
Rich Products
River Holding Corp.
Robert Mitchell Co., Inc.
Rockwell Automations
Rockwell Collins
Rogers
Rohm & Haas
Ropak Northwest
RR Donnelley & Sons
Rugged Sportswear
Russell Corporation

S
S1 Corporation
S & B Engineers and Constructors
Sabre
Safeway
SAIC
Sallie Mae
Samsonite
Samuel-Whittar, Inc.
Sanford
Sanmina-SCI
Sapient
Sara Lee
Saturn Electronics & Engineering
SBC Communications
Schumacher Electric
Scientific Atlanta
Seal Glove Manufacturing
Seco Manufacturing Co.
SEI Investments
Sequa Corporation
Seton Company
Sheldahl Inc.
Shipping Systems, Inc.
Siebel Systems
Sierra Atlantic

Sights Denim Systems, Inc.
Signal Transformer
Signet Armorlite, Inc
Sikorsky
Silicon Graphics
Simula Automotive SafetyÊ
SITEL
Skyworks Solutions
SMC Networks
SML Labels
SNC Manufacturing CompanyÊ
SoftBrands
Sola Optical USA
Solectron
Sonoco Products Co.
Southwire Company
Sovereign Bancorp
Spectrum Control
Spicer Driveshaft Manufacturing
Springs Industries
Springs Window Fashions
Sprint
Sprint PCS
SPX Corporation
Square D
Standard Textile Co.
Stanley Furniture
Stanley Works
Stant Manufacturing
Starkist Seafood
State Farm Insurance
State Street
Steelcase
StorageTek
StrategicPoint Investment Advisors
Strattec Security Corp.
STS Apparel Corporation
Summitville Tiles
Sun Microsystems

Sunrise Medical
SunTrust Banks
Superior Uniform Group
Supra Telecom
Sure Fit
SurePrep
The Sutherland Group
Sweetheart Cup Co.
Swift Denim
Sykes Enterprises
Symbol Technologies
Synopsys
Synygy

T
Takata Retraint Systems
Target
Teccor Electronics
Techalloy Company, Inc.
Technotrim
Tecumseh
Tee Jays Manufacturing
Telcordia
Telect
Teleflex
TeleTech
Telex Communications
Tellabs
Tenneco Automotive
Teradyne
Texaco Exploration and Production
Texas Instruments
Textron
Thermal Industries
Therm-O-Disc, Inc.
Thomas & Betts
Thomasville Furniture
Thomas Saginaw Ball Screw Co.
Three G's Manufacturing Co.

Thrivent Financial for Lutherans
Time Warner
Tingley Rubber Corp.
The Timken Company
The Toro Company
Tomlinson Industries
Tower Automotive
Toys "R" Us
Trailmobile Trailer
Trans-Apparel Group
TransPro, Inc.
Trans Union
Travelocity
Trek Bicycle Corporation
Trend Technologies
TriMas Corp.
Trinity Industries
Triquint Semiconductor
TriVision Partners
Tropical Sportswear
TRW Automotive
Tumbleweed Communications
Tupperware
Tyco Electronics
Tyco International

U
UCAR Carbon Company
Underwriters Laboratories
UniFirst Corporation
Union Pacific Railroad
Unison Industries
Unisys
United Airlines
UnitedHealth Group Inc.
United Online
United Plastics Group
United States Ceramic Tile
United Technologies

Universal Lighting Technologies
USAA

V
Valence Technology
Valeo Climate Control
VA Software
Velvac
Vertiflex Products
Veritas
Verizon
VF Corporation
Viasystems
Vishay
Visteon
VITAL Sourcing

W
Wabash Alloys, L.L.C.
Wabash Technologies
Wachovia Bank
Walgreens
Walls Industries
Warnaco
Washington Group International
Washington Mutual
WebEx
WellChoice
Wellman Thermal Systems

Walls Industries
Werner Co.
West Corporation
Weavexx
Weiser Lock
West Point Stevens
Weyerhaeuser
Whirlpool
White Rodgers
Williamson-Dickie Manufacturing
Company
Winpak Films
Wolverine World Wide
Woodstock Wire Works
WorldCom
World Kitchen
Wyeth
Wyman-Gordon Forgings

X Y Z
Xerox
Xpectra Incorporated
Xpitax
Yahoo!
Yarway Corporation
York International
Zenith
ZettaWorks

Global Workforce Report: Emerging Markets--Expanding the Frontier

What about Texas Instruments building a new $1 billion state of the art semiconductor chip testing and assembly plant in the Philippines?

This new facility will add 3,000 workers to their global workforce of 31,000. One third of this workforce is based in Asia. Wouldn't it have been much better for America to have these 31,000 jobs in the American workforce? America should pass legislation to create a tariff on all worker compensation that is paid to a foreign country. If Texas Instruments saves 50% on labor cost then have the tariff at 100% of the amount of wages paid to the Philippines. On top of that Texas Instruments is taking $1 billion out of the economy of the United States to build the facility. We sure could have used those construction jobs in America. That type of corporate behavior should be condemned by all Americans.

The Philippines now rivals India for BPO investment and leads Southeast Asia in call center growth. Vietnam successfully competes against both China and India for software development centers and pharmaceutical facilities. Bangladesh is pulling light industry out of India and China, and Turkey is beating out Eastern Europe for auto assembly.

This movement of jobs overseas was created by Goldman Sachs in 2005 so that these developing countries become major economies. How can anyone support Goldman Sachs when they are promoting the shipment of American jobs to other countries? That doesn't seem very American to me? Then our government's leaders cater to their every need. The countries that Goldman Sachs wanted to transfer jobs to included the following; Egypt, Indonesia, Iran, South Korea, Mexico, Nigeria, Philippines, Vietnam, Bangladesh, Turkey and Pakistan. Why would we want to help the majority of these countries? The majority of them do not like America.

The capital-intensive semiconductor industry has moved out of the United States and into the emerging nations of Asia primarily because lower tax rates and other government incentives have reduced the cost of capital in those countries. In the semiconductor industry, the 80 percent differential in wage rates between the United States and emerging Asia results in less than a 10 percent difference in final costs, according to the Semiconductor Industry Association. What the United States government needs to do is tax these corporations to the extent that it is not beneficial to do business in a foreign country. "Made in the USA"

Intel has moved much of their packaging facility and production to Vietnam. The Intel plant was in the same $1 billion construction range. How can this type of company justify their lack of support for the American people and then expect the people to purchase their products?

Texas Instruments stated that they will have no difficulty in filling the 3,000 positions at the new plant because we have a hiring process that begins with cooperation with 26 universities all over the Philippines. Texas Instruments should develop the same type of agreements with the United States universities that they are using to find employees in the Philippines. Texas Instruments could develop a program with the American universities that would include a six month training program sponsored by the university and then these participants would have a job when they graduate. That program would be much better than the students of today graduating without any hope of finding a good job.

Hexaware Technologies Ltd., a global service company has over 5,700 employees in different locations in several different countries. Hesaware is expanding their facilities in Mexico and anticipates the hiring of an additional 200 employees. Many of the prospective employees have studied in the United States. If they have received their education in the United States why don't they become American citizens and work in America?

Though some American firms are bringing overseas work back home, evidence is growing that companies are moving more jobs than ever to China and other countries. This trend could have serious effects on reducing the unemployment rate in the United States.

The most recent Commerce Department data show that employment at the foreign subsidiaries and affiliates of U.S. multinational firms grew by 729,000 in two years, to 11.9 million in 2008 from 2006. Over that same period, domestic employment by such firms slipped by 500,000 jobs, to 21.1 million.

Some of the American companies that have moved parts of their operations overseas are Hilton Worldwide Hotels, Hewlett Packard Co., J.P. Morgan and Chase Manhattan. These companies have moved their call centers overseas and the American's wonder why we can't understand a word when we talk to these call centers?

CHAPTER SEVEN:

The Show Me State

Missouri has been known as the show me state for as long as I can remember. What Missouri is showing the rest of the country is how to eliminate the problems with illegals?

Missouri has no illegals!

Why Missouri Has No Illegal Aliens!!!

Missouri's approach to the problem of illegal immigration appears to be more advanced, sophisticated, strict and effective than anything to date in Arizona. Do the loonies in San Francisco, or the White House, appreciate what Missouri has done? When are our fearless President and his dynamic Attorney General going to take action to require Missouri start accepting illegal immigrants once again?

So, why doesn't Missouri receive attention?

Answer: There are no Mexican illegals in Missouri to demonstrate.

The "Show Me" state has once again showed us how it should be done.

There needs to be more publicity and exposure regarding what Missouri has done.

In 2007, Missouri placed on the ballot a proposed constitutional amendment designating English as the official language of Missouri. 90% of the voters in Missouri voted in favor of the new law. Thus English became the official language for all governmental activity in Missouri.

No individual has the right to demand government services in a language other than English. In 2008 a measure was passed that required the Missouri Highway Patrol and other law enforcement officials to verify the immigration status of any person arrested, and inform federal authorities if the person is found to be in Missouri illegally. Missouri law enforcement offices receive specific training with respect to enforcement of federal immigration laws.

In Missouri illegal immigrants do not have access to taxpayer's benefits such as food stamps and health care through Missouri HealthNET. In 2009 a measure was passed that ensures Missouri's public institutions of higher education do not award financial aid to individuals who are illegally in the United States.

In Missouri all post-secondary institutions of higher education to annually certify to the Missouri Department of Higher Education that they have not knowingly awarded financial aid to students who are unlawfully present in the United States.

So while Arizona has made national news for its new law, it is important to remember Missouri has been far more proactive in addressing this horrific problem.

Missouri has made it clear that illegal immigrants are not welcome in the state and they will certainly not receive public benefits at the expense of Missouri taxpayers.

See, article in "The Ozarks Sentinel" Editorial Opinion - Nita Jane Ayres, May 13, 2010.

Missouri Voters Enact English-Only Law Posted on: 2008-11-11 00:07:43

"Missouri has always been known as a bellwether state," said Mauro E. Mujica, Chairman of the Board of United States English, Inc. "This vote by the people of Missouri is a message to the nation that whether in cities, suburbs or rural America, Democratic, Republican or Independent, we are united as a country in favor of an official language."

The Missouri ballot initiative marks the ninth time in nine attempts where voters have approved making English the official language of the state or strengthening the existing laws. Prior to the successful initiative in Missouri, voters had previously approved an official English ballot initiative in Arizona (2006), Utah (2000), Alaska (1998), Colorado (1988), Alabama (1988), Florida (1988), Arizona (1988) and California (1986). To date 30 states have made English the official language of the state.

Now the federal government needs to enact the same laws.

CHAPTER EIGHT:

Safety on Our Southern Border

The risk of living on the southern border of the United States grows with each passing day. When is the government going to do something to protect our borders?

The border between El Paso, Texas and Juarez, Mexico took the lives to two students that were attending the University of Texas El Paso. These were Americans whose lives straddled the border, business students attending classes at the University of Texas at El Paso but living in Ciudad Juarez amid family and friends.

They had been on their campus, a peaceful enclave of grassy plazas flanked by breathtaking desert mountains, just hours before they were gunned down last week in Juarez, their car riddled with bullets as they headed home.

Commuting from Mexico to the United States was as natural to them as taking the Holland Tunnel from New Jersey into New York. It's a life many border residents continue to embrace even as the death toll from the drug war in Mexico continues to rise.

The United States State Department says more than 80 Americans have been killed this year in Chihuahua, the state where Juarez is located. That's already more than the 79 homicides of United States citizens in all of Mexico in 2009.

An international business major rides a bus to the border, walks across the bridge over the Rio Grande, then hops another bus to campus, a process that takes 45 minutes and would be longer if he did not use the faster moving immigration lines for Americans. Students who drive across the border daily say they often must endure lines of an hour or more. This student was mugged outside his family's home last year but still says he'd rather reside in Juarez than El Paso.

Americans killed in Mexico have tended to be people who cross back and forth regularly. Some were with Mexican friends or relatives who were the targets. Others were hit by stray bullets.

The border has become complicated, and it becomes difficult for people going back and forth. Juarez is a city held hostage by a nearly three year battle for control of drug smuggling routes between the cartel bearing the city's name and the Sinaloa cartel. More than 6,500 people have been killed there since the start of 2008. Across the country, more than 33,000 people have been killed in drug violence since President Felipe Calderon launched his national assault on organized crime in late 2006.

Even as the U.S. government warns citizens not to travel to Juarez, there are on average around 85,000 people coming and going every day, according to United States Customs and Border Protection. An agency's spokesman in El Paso noted that many people in the area have strong ties on both sides of the border.

One of the students that were attending the University of Texas El Paso made the comment that just because he was born in the United States but he really is a Mexican. America needs to wake up and understand that these illegal Mexican babies that are born in the United States do not feel that they are American. You can't be Mexican and American at the same time. Do you pledge allegiance to this country? Have you always gone to American schools? You have enjoyed the freedom of America yet you tout Mexico as the greatest place of all. I wish the government would gather up all the illegal Mexicans and every other person who is not a citizen that are here illegally and take them back to their country where they belong no matter where that country is located. America did not kill your citizens but Mexicans have killed Americans making them the bad guys not us. Go home I say to all illegals that are here. Our country would be so much better off without the illegal immigrants. There would be jobs and all our resources like welfare food stamps health programs and education programs would improve. They have been so inflated that every state in this country is hurting really bad.

Americans that are killed in Mexico are simply rolling the dice and may come up short. Anyone who can read much less being a college student should know the risks these days of traveling to and through Mexico especially near the United States border so although it is a shame it is not all that unexpected. Until Mexico starts to control their side of the border the Mexicans will continue to get killed and that is the way it will be. In the meantime increased border control and protection must be established to keep the rift raft south of the United States border.

When we have complete safety on our Mexican border we will have accomplished an important part of "My American Dream". There will not be a safe border until the fence and America's highway are completed. It is not possible to enforce our immigration laws when we let a million illegals cross over the border into the United States per year.

Sharron Angle the Republican challenger of Senator Harry Reid in Nevada aired an ad depicting immigrants as violent gang members who are "forcing families to live in fear." The ad criticizes Reid for voting against declaring English the national language in the United States and for siding with President Obama in stopping Arizona's tough new immigration law.

The families in the ad who are "living in fear" are white and the children who must live without a national language are white as well. However, the immigrants depicted are being arrested, have tattoos and are wearing bandanas, symbolizing their participation in a gang. It ends by saying: "Harry Reid, it's clear whose side he's on and it's not ours."

Texas Sheriff Warns Colorado Officers about Border

Zapata County Sheriff Sigi Gonzalez said he has been pressing since at least 2005 for more federal help to protect residents on the Mexican border who are afraid of going on their own land after dark, as the sounds of rocket propelled grenades and gunfire have become more familiar.

On the border, people live in fear on the United States side. On the Mexico side, forget it. It's totally out of control. Or I should say, it's in the control of the drug cartels.

Hartley, who grew up in Loveland, said she is speaking up about violence on the border on behalf of her own family but also for other victims with relatives in Mexico who have stayed silent for fear of retaliation.

"Ultimately, this is bigger than just David. His death will not be in vain because I will continue to do what I can to secure our border," she said.

Pirates have robbed several Americans on Falcon Lake this year. Though the Hartleys had been living in Reynoso, Mexico, and then McAllen, Texas, Hartley said she hadn't realized the breadth of violence perpetrated by Mexican drug cartels until she and her husband were targeted.

The cartels have pushed into the United States too. A 2008 report from the National Drug Intelligence Center shows Mexican drug trafficking organizations have operations in at least 195 United States cities, including five in Colorado and cities in Alaska and Hawaii.

Organizers of the session said they had asked Gonzalez to speak before the Hartley case began. Gonzalez says he regularly speaks around the country about border issues.

DANGER – PUBLIC WARNING
TRAVEL NOT RECOMMENDED

- **Active Drug and Human Smuggling Area**

- **Visitors May Encounter Armed and Smuggling Vehicles Traveling at High Rates of Speed**

- **Stay Away From Trash, Clothing, Backpacks, and Abandoned Vechicles**

- **If You See Suspicious Activity, <u>Do Not Confront</u> Move Away and Call 911**

- **BLM Encourages Visitors To Use Public Lands North to Interstate 8.**

The sign above is the federal government's answer to securing the borders

The federal government does not have any sense what so ever. They are so blind when it concerns something that the vast majority of the American citizens really care about. How many American citizens have to be murdered in Mexico before the President stops suing Arizona and starts enforcing the federal laws regarding illegals? Has the President ever read any part of our immigration laws or the Constitution?

The United States has thousands of military personnel stationed close to the border and yet he is too stupid to use any of them to protect our country. The President would rather bow down to Calderon than stand up for the American citizens. The military has the technology to locate every drug cartel stronghold and eliminate it within 24 hours. What is the reason that the President will not do anything to address our border problems? We need to load the weapons and fire at will on every drug cartel. They are killing the Americans with their constant flow of illegals and drugs. It would be so simple even a caveman could do it.

While this war against the American citizens is continuing to escalate President Obama is letting Mexico and Latin American countries bring litigation against Arizona for trying to protect its borders and citizens. Our own Executive department will not even enforce our immigration laws. We have a group of legislators in the federal government that are just as much criminals as the killers attacking our citizens in Mexico. The federal government refuses to enforce the immigration laws. They refuse to enact any legislation that will secure our border and stop the flow of illegals into our country. Arizona stands on the front lines of defense and should be hailed be every American.

Barack Obama and his minions litigate Arizona into federal magistrate's court and later the World Court. It should be no mystery. Barack Obama and most of those who voted for him have a psychological hatred for this country.

Just remember if the great state of Arizona can be litigated into a magistrate's court then any other state that runs afoul of these loose cannons can also be hauled into court.

The President of Mexico had the audacity to come to the United States of America and tell us that we are treating his illegal immigrants badly? And what's worse is that our President Obama was right there and stood before the cameras with him and didn't stand up to the Mexican President's criticism about our country.

The Federal government sued Arizona over SB1070. Close our border to everyone until our people are all back to work and our country is up and running like it should be. All welfare recipients must do the jobs the illegals do, or they do not get a welfare check, what do we need illegals here for anyway. Make the welfare people work for their check. No freebies. The taxpayers are paying the bill and everyone needs to understand that there are no free lunches. Freedom is not free. Everyone pays a price.

What we have here is the failure of President Obama to realize that Arizona is not the enemy, but Mexico is. Shut the boarder down with Mexico using the Marines at Camp Pendleton, California. Give the Mexicans 30 day notice, and then shoot the illegal aliens, drug runners, and terrorists on sight. These Mexican drug lords are bringing drugs right into your homes and schools, and recruiting your kids to sell drugs. The illegals are bleeding our nation dry with them taking advantage of our system. In the meantime the terrorists are sneaking dirty weapons or possibly atomic bombs into the United States. While all this is going on President Obama is sitting on his hands suing Arizona because they want to check ID's?

We are so worried about terrorists overseas when we have terrorist right next door in Mexico. Put up a DMZ zone between the United States and Mexico. Mexican Cartel: terrorists who behead politicians and law enforcement. Mexican Cartel: terrorists involved in illegal activities to raise money. Mexican Cartel: terrorists who hold hostages to achieve power and kill hostages to create fear Mexican Cartel: terrorists who kill innocent women and children claiming territories. Mexican Cartel: terrorists who control their government through fear. Mexican Cartel: terrorists involved in illegal drug production and distribution. Mexican Cartel: terrorists who kidnap, torture and rape. Mexican Cartel: terrorists who threaten neighboring countries. Mexican Cartel: terrorists who cause mass exodus of refugees seeking safety. Mexican Cartel: terrorists who control the media reporting by killing reporters.

The police stopped at a Home Depot yesterday. They confronted 15 Mexican day laborers. They told them that if they were harassed by people suggesting that they were illegal they should call the police. They would come out and help them. They should not concern themselves about being deported. The police are here to help them. This is totally out of control. Now they are called day laborers instead of illegals. Give me a break and send them all back to where they came from.

There are over 200,000 Mexican nationals living in garages in Los Angeles, and paying no taxes, but collecting social benefits. Pelosi is quoted as saying, "it's cheaper to let them come in illegally than to build a barrier to keep them out". It's no wonder California is bankrupt.

It is a scary thought that there are 20,000,000 plus illegals in this country that we know nothing about their history or past. We have been invaded and the federal government has turned its back on the citizens of these United States. The President needs to wake up and smell the roses.

The people that are living near the border will tell you that we need a real fence. These people have no conscience and we let them freely come to our country. The current administration has no clue, sitting 2,000 miles away in their cushy White House offices or traveling all over the country to campaign. I believe every voting citizen of the United States should be voting against anyone that is against preserving the United States and the Constitution. Protect all the people of our nation and send those back that do not want to come here legally and embrace our great nation. Apply for citizenship and become a true American.

We had better start paying attention to our Mexican border, not only for illegal immigration, but for these thugs and terrorist that are killing in Mexico and kidnapping and killing throughout the southwest United States. Bring our troops home from the Middle East and protect our borders with military might.

CHAPTER NINE:

Unfinished Business

The Democrats were so anxious to get on the campaign trail that they left lots of unfinished business that should have been dealt with in both houses of Congress.

10 UNFINISHED BILLS LEFT BY PELOSI & REID

The Democrats are so scared of losing control of the House and Senate in the midterm elections, that they are packing up & leaving D.C. to spend more time on the campaign trail.

The American people have an absentee Congress, whose leaders choose politics over getting work done. The top 10 most important pieces of legislation left unfinished by the do-nothing Congress led by Pelosi & Reid include:

1. CUT TAXES: Thanks to the Democrats every American will pay more taxes on January1 2010. Pelosi refuses to bring a vote to the House floor to extend Bush tax cuts, which expire at the end of the year. Pelosi's own party turned against her, with many House Democrats pushing for a vote on tax rates before they face the voters in November. In the Senate, Reid is also denying a vote on extending the lower tax

rates established in 2001 and 2003. Reid claims the tax rate extension legislation will be brought up during the lame-duck session after the election.

2. CREATE JOBS: Obama's $800 billion stimulus bill has been an epic failure. Unemployment in the U.S. is 9.6% & unemployment claims went up again in August, proving that Obama's "Summer of Recovery" was political rhetoric. To create jobs, Congress must cut taxes & government mandates (like Obamacare) on small businesses owners, who will then start hiring again. Reid's home state of Nevada has the highest unemployment rate in the United States.

3. MAKE A BUDGET: The Democrats & Obama have not passed a budget this year to determine government spending. The inability of Pelosi & Reid to get enough votes to pass their budget is indicative of the unpopularity of their big government spending policies. The United States economy is a mess and the Democrats can't even pass a budget to plan for spending.

4. APPROPRIATIONS BILLS: The Democratic-controlled Congress has not passed any of the 12 annual appropriations bills for fiscal 2011. The bills are withering in committees.

5. TRADE: The Chamber of Commerce is urging Congress to renew the Generalized System of Preferences (GSP) and the Andean Trade Preference Act (ATPA) before they expire at the end of the year. The chamber, wrote to members of Congress that "GSP boosts the competitiveness of United States manufacturers and lowers the cost of consumer goods for American families. Moving GSP imports from the docks to the retail shelves supports tens of thousands of United States jobs.

6. STOP THE EPA: The Environmental Protection Agency (EPA) is planning to bypass Congress & dictate rules to curb carbon gas emission. Reid refuses to schedule a vote on the bill.

7. REPEAL OBAMACARE'S TAX BURDEN: Small businesses are suffering under the Obamacare mandate to file a 1099 tax form to any vendor paid over $600 in a year. Over 40 million small businesses are

required to file these new tax reports for healthcare. Despite bipartisan support for repealing this Obamacare tax burden on employers, both the House & Senate have dithered.

8. SECURE OUR BORDERS: Reid has made immigration reform a top priority of his leadership in the Senate and has accomplished nothing.

9. PORK SPENDING REFORM: Pelosi promised to "bring transparency and openness to the budget process and to the use of earmarks." Reid asserted that "the days of unlimited and unaccountable congressionally directed spending are gone." But the Democratic leaders have consistently passed legislation laden with pork-barrel spending to benefit their home districts.

10. ETHICS TRIALS FOR RANGEL & WATERS: House Ethics Committee charged Democrats Rangel with 13 ethical violations and Waters with 3 counts of ethical charges. The Rangel and Waters trials have been scheduled since the charges were announced. All 5 Republican members of the committee called on the committee's chairwoman Zoe Lofgren (D-CA) to schedule trials for Rangel and Waters before the Nov. elections. Lofgren refuses to schedule the trials.

CHAPTER TEN:

Obama Begging For Votes

During the last days of the mid-term elections President Obama continued his campaigning gusto covering several states in pursuit of some Democratic votes. The President has attacked the Republican Party with causing the economic problems that the country is facing.

Begging will not get the votes for the Democratic Party. President Obama by your actions for the last two years has given the voters all the information on you and your agenda and frankly the voters do not like your agenda. As President you lied numerous times right to our faces so just don't get settled into the White House because you will not be staying for another term.

He continues to say that the Republicans had driven the economy into a ditch and then stood by and criticized while Democrats have pulled it out. The President must be reading the main stream media's articles stating that the recession ended over a year ago. Now that progress has been made, he said, "We can't have special interests groups sitting shotgun. We gotta have middle class families up in front. We don't mind the Republicans joining us. They can come for the ride, but they gotta sit in back." Now let me tell you that I am not an English major but the President of the United States using the term "gotta" is pretty lame for someone pressing for better education. Then to make a comment that they can sit in the back is kind of like the days when the blacks were required to sit in the back of the buss. These comments are from the President of the United States. Our President is one big racist.

If you have to try hard to persuade people to vote for you then you must know your not doing your job. The job isn't going to get done by blaming Bush for everything. Obama is the president now and it's his job to make it better and not make it worse. He is supposed to be our leader and the only thing he is doing is leading us backwards. I see him on the news channels or on a trip more than I see him at the empty desk in the White House. It would seem like the President should be spending more time addressing the pressing problems of the country? How about devoting some time to securing our borders or working on the unemployment problem? Which reminds me who is paying for all of these campaign trips? Is the Democratic Party going to reimburse the government?

I realize that some or all of the citizens are aware of the following facts. They just bear repeating for those that have forgotten or for those that didn't know. The day that the Democratic Party took control of the Congress was actually January 3, 2007 and not on January 22, 2009. The last two years of the Bush administration was controlled by the Democratic Congress.

That was the first time that the Democratic Party controlled a majority in both chambers of Congress since the 103rd Congress in 1995. Now for all of those that like to bash Bush's economic policies remember that the unemployment rate when Bush left office was at 4.6%. That is compared to the Obama administrations policies that have had the unemployment rate at 9.6% or higher for the last year. President Bush's economic policies had created new jobs for a record 52 straight months. On January 3, 2007 was the day that Barney Frank took over the House Financial Services Committee. We all know what has happened to the housing market during his tenure at that position. Chris Dodd took over the Senate Banking Committee. After these two gained control the economic meltdown happened in 15 months.

The country can thank the Democratic controlled Congress for adding $5 to $6 trillion to the federal deficit since they have been in control. President Bush asked the Democratic Congress on 17 different occasions to stop the Fannie Mae and Freddie Mac's lending policies because they would financially ruin the United States. Nobody would listen and now the Democrats are blaming

Bush when in reality they were the ones that caused the financial meltdown. Bush may have been in the car, but the Democrats were in charge of the gas pedal and steering wheel they were driving.

That should set the record straight on the Bush administration. So, as you listen to all the commercials and media from the Democrats who are now distancing themselves from their voting record and their party, remember how they didn't listen to you when you said you didn't want all the bailouts, you didn't want the health care bill, you didn't want cap and trade, you didn't want them to continue spending money we don't have.

Attacking Republicans with dirty campaign policies is all that the Democrats have to run on. They sure can't run on their record of how they ran government when they controlled the White House, the House of Representatives, and the Senate. The Democrats sure can't run on more failed promises like the last few years. They have absolutely nothing to make their constituents want to vote for them so they have to sling dirt. They have spread enough manure to cover every field in the Midwest.

President Obama slams race, insults Americans and his aunt is as arrogant as the President. Obama's aunt came to the United States as an illegal and demands citizenship and is on welfare. Would he help her out no he didn't he would not give her a penny because why should he give her any of his loot when we can give her the governments money. The President then tells the American people that some of us should ride in the back of the bus. Do you believe this President? Does any one wonder why the President will not do anything to stop the flow of illegals into the United States? Does any one else believe that the President really wants to give amnesty to all of the 20 million illegals that are already here?

President Obama you continue to spread your rhetoric about how the Republicans haven't compromised on any of the major issues. Would it be too much for you to look at the definition of compromise? Apparently the President thinks that compromise means that everyone must agree with him. It would be nice if the President would get over his arrogance just once.

The Obama administration is making good on an election-year promise to Arkansas Senator Blanche Lincoln to give millions of dollars in aid to big agribusiness supporters of Blanche Lincoln is a Democrat from Arkansas.

Democrat Senator Blanche Lincoln, caught in a bruising race for re-election, made a deal with White House chief of staff Rahm Emanuel when she sold her vote for Obamacare. The Agriculture Department took almost two months to figure out how to make the off-the-books payment, since such aid is usually subject to congressional approval.

Agriculture Secretary Tom Vilsack announced last Wednesday that the $630 million in pay-offs will come from money at the USDA was to be used to buy food for poor American infants and children in the Supplement School Nutrition programs. According to the Obama administration and Senator Lincoln, this year the hungry just have to do without. Hey Blanche how many children will go hungry to buy your Senate seat? The people of Arkansas must be proud.

President Obama is great politician. Bush was not. President Bush was a great president. Obama is not. It's that simple.

Do we want a leader or a follower? Do we want someone apparently more interested in following trends, in appearing on talk shows, comedy shows, getting his face and family on magazine covers, hosting party after party or do we want a president who leads? We've all heard President Obama say, "the mess my administration inherited". He's said it many, many times. I challenge anyone out there to find a single quote, a sound byte of any occurrence at all of President Bush saying that about the Clinton administration, particularly after 9/11. Obama chose the correct analogy. It is a deep hole to climb out of. You won't. Why? Because President Bush didn't blame others for the mess he was in. He took responsibility. He was a president, not an appeaser to polls, pundits or talk shows. He was a leader. He was fallible and human, but he was a leader.

President Obama needs to stop blaming others. He needs to take responsibility for his presidency, as Bush did, as Clinton did, and Reagan before him. He is responsible for the state of the economy, for national defense, for the welfare and safety of all Americans, not just those on the left. He needs to get out of campaign mode and be a President to the nation, not just to one side, to one race, to one voting block.

Before anything else, he needs to stop blaming the Bush administration for the economy right now. Why? Because not only is it a sign of weak leadership to blame others, but in this case, it's completely inaccurate.

Everyone who has any knowledge at all about the economy knows that the Democrats took control of congress in 2007, which is when the economy took a nosedive. Even SNL in their original skit (before it was censored) praised Bush for repeatedly warning the Frank and Dodd about Fannie May and Freddie Mac. The fact that it was even written on SNL is a miracle in itself. Ignoring the facts and continuing to blame a previous administration or his present opposition will only sink him deeper into the hole he mentions.

The hole is not the economy and it's not even the war or 9/11. The hole is the mood of the American people. Obama was elected for the sole purpose of change, changing our mood as a nation. Bringing us together again, all parties, all peoples. How's he doing? With his approval rating going into the tank it doesn't look like the American people think he is doing too good of a job?

Democrats relied on more than the President's time to boost their chances in the final days of the campaign. There was the matter of federal funds, too, in the form of hundreds of millions in grants announced during the day to provide high speed rail service in California, between Chicago and Iowa, and elsewhere. Administration officials left it to Democratic lawmakers to make the announcements, and they did, stressing the job-creating potential of the expansions.

Democrats hastened to Reid's side in Nevada. Sen. John Kerry, D-Mass., became the latest lawmaker to send out an urgent e-mail fundraising appeal for the top Democrat.

It said the same wealthy Texans who attacked his Vietnam War record during the 2004 presidential campaign were now aiming at Reid. "These guys will say anything and spend anything to get what they want," Kerry wrote.

Here is some news that is going to be hard to believe. The President is returning to the White House for a few days before returning to the campaigning trail. What a change for our President. Going to the White House for some rest and planning of his next vacation.

Every election time for the last 50 years the Democrats threaten the elderly and disabled by saying the Republicans are going to take away their social security when the truth is that it is the Democrats who have been stealing your social security.

Q: Which Party denied a Social Security cost of living expense raise to the elderly and disabled 2 years in a row?

A: It was the Democrat party under Barrack Obama in 2010 and 2011.

Q: Which Political Party took Social Security from the independent 'Trust Fund' and put it into the general fund so that Congress could spend it?

A: It was Lyndon Johnson and the Leftist Progressive Democrat controlled House and Senate.

Q: Which Political Party eliminated the income tax deduction for Social Security (FICA) withholding?

A: The Leftist Progressive Democrat Party.

Q: Which Political Party started taxing Social Security annuities?

A: The Leftist Progressive Democrat Party, with Al Gore casting the 'tie-breaking' deciding vote as President of the Senate, while he was Vice President of the United States.

Q: Which Political Party decided to start giving annuity payments to immigrants?

A: That's right! Jimmy Carter and the Leftist Progressive Democrat Party. Beginning at age 65, immigrants began to receive Social Security payments even if they never worked. The Leftist Progressive Democrat Party gave these payments to them, even though they never paid a dime into social security.

Since many of us have paid into social security for years and are now receiving a social security check every month -- and then finding that we are getting taxed on 85% of the money we paid to the federal government to put away.

Then, after violating the original contract (FICA), the Leftist Progressive Democrats turn around and tell you that the Republicans want to take your Social Security away.

And the worst part about it is uninformed citizens believe it!

This is a huge admission made by Obama when he thought only his "friends" were listening. It was tailored for a specific audience – not you and me and the vast majority of Americans who want to keep their nation free and secure. Of course, it's racist to the core.

This action by Obama was specifically directed at Hispanics. Who are their enemies in America? Presumably anyone who wants to see our immigration laws enforced. It's racist just to assume that all Hispanic-Americans want to see open borders. It's certainly not true. But, as you prepare to go to the polls I want you to internalize this statement from Obama. "We're going to punish our enemies." Maybe we ought to turn the tables on Obama. Maybe that should be motivation for his enemies to turn out in record numbers.

Maybe the hard-working, law-abiding citizens of the country Obama hates will finally have the motivation and clarity they need to punish him and his party of anti-American zealots hell-bent on destroying the foundations of the greatest experiment in liberty the world has ever known.

According to President Obama Americans are confused, angry, scared, uncertain, anxious, frustrated, nervous, discouraged, shaken up and clearly do not think clearly. The only people that think clearly are the lemmings that believe every word that Obama says.

President Obama states that the American citizen would be more inclined to believe and support his policies if the Republican Party would not spread so much gloom and distrust concerning his policies. This is the same President that will not take the blame for any of his actions or their outcome. When will the President stop blaming other people for his failures?

Obama sometimes talks about voters' anger being misplaced, suggesting it should be directed at Republicans instead of him. He accuses the Republican Party of fomenting voter anger by refusing to help solve problems in Washington, and then of seeking to capitalize on continued hurt over the economy come Election Day.

What had Reagan accomplished, two years into his term? When did you hear him blame Carter or the democratically controlled congress? Obama has a congress controlled by Democrats and he can't get anything done. The President is a pathetic excuse for a leader.

This would be funny if it weren't so insulting. We don't like the President's policies, so there's something wrong with our logic.

Granted we disagree. We don't like socialism. We don't want amnesty for any illegals. We want our border secured. We want Muslim terrorists called Muslim terrorists instead of militants. The President caters to the Muslims, wants amnesty for all illegals and he likes socialism. Besides that the President couldn't care less about securing the borders. Maybe we should call the President's thinking confused.

The following are some comments made by American citizens regarding President Obama. They are not in any particular order just as I received them. You will agree with some and disagree with others. They are only included to make people think.

Could it be that President has Narcissistic personality disorde0? The symptoms may include:

* Believing that you're better than others
* Fantasizing about power, success and attractiveness
* Exaggerating your achievements or talents
* Expecting constant praise and admiration
* Believing that you're special and acting accordingly
* Failing to recognize other people's emotions and feelings
* Expecting others to go along with your ideas and plans
* Taking advantage of others
* Expressing disdain for those you feel are inferior
* Being jealous of others

* Believing that others are jealous of you
* Trouble keeping healthy relationships
* Setting unrealistic goals
* Being easily hurt and rejected
* Having a fragile self-esteem
* Appearing as tough-minded or unemotional

Obama sounds and looks pretty depraved these days. Now he's projecting his feelings onto the American people. I think it's time to take this man out of the White House. He is not mentally or emotionally healthy enough to execute the duties of the President. I think the strain is getting to him.

After all, he did abandon his duties to flit across the country on the taxpayer's dollar to campaign for the Democratic Party. That in itself shows that he is not capable of caring out the oath that he took. He does not represent all of the people as a President should, he just represents his Democratic Party, the illegal aliens, the Hispanics, the gays, the Muslims but not the American people. Get rid of him.

Who does this idiot think he is telling us we are confused and not thinking clearly? This guy is a loon. He needs to start packing right now and get the hell out of Dodge. In my 60 years I have never seen such a sad excuse for a human as this one. Take into consideration that Hitler was before my time. This man is another Hitler though. We cannot put up with this as a nation. He has got to go. I want my freedoms back and I want my country back. This is the Home of the Brave and the Land of the Free. Let's show this idiot our bravery and get our freedom back before it is all gone! God have mercy on our souls if we don't! God bless the USA!

I want to know two things. First: who is paying the tab to have Obama fly all over America to campaign for the Democrats? Second: with all that is wrong in the country with the economy, joblessness, people losing their homes, etc, why isn't the President in DC doing some work to get us back up and running instead of playing the country's psychiatrist?

Do the people that show up at his rallies even still listen to this clown? He should've been impeached by now for his treasonous acts against America. Now he's trying to make us out to be the weak nut cases because we don't agree with his unfair and disastrous change? Get this guy out of office.

After reading some of the citizen's comments it becomes apparent that a lot of Americans are not happy with the actions and results of the President.

A Different Slant on the Obama Presidency

This person's slant turns into a great message of hope! Why does it take an eighty-year-old to put it in perspective?

One eighty-year-old lady loves Obama and she may have a very good point. She says that Obama is amazing, and is rebuilding the American dream! She gives us an entirely new slant on the "amazing" job Obama is doing, and she says that she will thank God for the president. Keep reading for her additional comments and an explanation. When discussing Obama, she says:

1. Obama destroyed the Clinton Political Machine, driving a stake through the heart of Hillary's presidential aspirations something no Republican was ever able to do.

2. Obama killed off the Kennedy Dynasty no more Kennedy's trolling Washington looking for booze and no more women wanting rides home or driving lessons.

3. Obama is destroying the Democratic Party before our eyes. Dennis Moore had never lost a race. Evan Bayh had never lost a race. Byron Dorgan had never lost a race. Harry Reid hopefully soon to be gone! These are just a handful of the Democrats whose political careers Obama has destroyed. By the end of 2010, dozens more will be gone. Just think, in December of 2008 the Democrats were on the rise. In the last two election cycles, they had picked up fourteen Senate seats and fifty-two House seats. The press was touting the death of the Conservative Movement and the Republican Party. However, in just one year, Obama put a stop to all of this and will probably give the House -- if not the Senate -- back to the Republicans.

4.   Obama has completely exposed liberals and progressives for what they are. Sadly, every generation seems to need to re-learn the lesson on why they should never actually put liberals in charge. Obama is bringing home the lesson very well: Liberals tax, borrow and spend. Liberals won't bring themselves to protect America. Liberals want to take over the economy. Liberals think they know what is best for everyone. Liberals are not happy until they are running your life.

5.   Obama has brought more Americans back to Conservatism than anyone since Reagan. In one year, he has rejuvenated the Conservative Movement and brought out to the streets millions of freedom-loving Americans. Name one other time when you saw your friends and neighbors this interested in taking back America?

6.   Obama, with his "amazing leadership," has sparked the greatest period of sales of firearms and ammunition this country has seen. Law abiding citizens have rallied and have provided a "stimulus" to the sporting goods field while other industries have failed, faded, or moved off-shore.

7.   In all honesty, one year ago I was more afraid than I have been in my life. Not afraid of the economy, but afraid of the direction our country was going. I thought, Americans have forgotten what this country is all about. My neighbors and friends, even strangers, have proved to me that my lack of confidence in the greatness and wisdom of the American people has been flat wrong.

8.   When the American people wake up, no smooth talking teleprompter reader can fool them. Barack Obama has served to wake up these great Americans. Again, I want to say: "Thank you, Barack Obama!" After all, this is exactly the kind of hope and change we desperately needed.

Does anyone remember that Obama had promised not to raise taxes on the citizens of the United States? There is legislation to impose a 1% transaction tax on everyone in America. The bill is HR-4646 and was introduced by Representative Peter DeFazio (D-OR) and Senator Tom Harkin (D-IA). The bill is not in committee and will probably not be brought out for vote until after the mid-term elections. The 1% transaction tax is proposed by President Obama's finance team and their plan is to sneak it in after the elections to keep it under the radar. This is a 1% tax on all transactions at any financial institution. That means all transactions including deposits at your bank, purchase of stocks, withdrawals from your bank and all transactions. This is from the President that promised that if you make under $250,000 per year you will not see one penny of new tax. Keep your eyes and ears open and you will be amazed at what you learn about our current administration. Well some will say it is only 1%. Just remember that once a tax is in place the rate can easily be raised.

Senator Reid has viewed the opinions of everyday American citizens with distain. He and Nancy Pelosi have been arrogant, condescending, and dismissive of what the people that put them in power wanted and did not want. We did not want to bail out the fat cat bankers, we did not want to bail out the fat cat union bosses (many did want to help workers in the auto industry), and we definitely did not want to pay extra to pay for health insurance for illegal aliens and deadbeats.

If the American citizens care about this nation and the quality of life that we will leave behind for our children, we had best make illegal immigration a priority for the next Presidential election. Both parties swept it under the rug in 2008. Neither side even discussed it in their debates. Stand up for border security now before it is too late.

It has been estimated by the Census Bureau that 9.7 million Hispanics voted in 2008. With the possibility of having 20 million illegals hoping for citizenship it becomes apparent why the Democrats want amnesty for these people. It is estimated that the Hispanic voters are about 70% Democratic.

The U.S. Commission on Civil Rights was set to vote on a 131-page draft report about the Obama administration's decision to drop the Black Panther voter intimidation case today — but a partisan Democratic member prevented the commission from doing its job. Michael Yaki walked out of the meeting before the vote, preventing the commission from reaching quorum, a procedural motion designed to stall for time. A report now seems unlikely to be released until after the midterm elections.

However, Talking Points Memo obtained a leaked copy of the report, which details credible allegations of Justice Department evasion, dissembling, and possible perjury before the commission. The document reveals a commission at the end of its rope dealing with a "recalcitrant" administration that refuses to investigate "serious allegations".

The draft report notes, "If the testimony before the Commission is true," the Justice Department's handling of the case would "encompass inappropriately selective enforcement of laws, harassment of dissenting employees, and alliances with outside interest groups, at odds with the rule of law."

CHAPTER ELEVEN:

The Pulse of America

This chapter is devoted to comments that have been made by Americans that are fed up with the policies of the Obama administration. Every comment comes from citizens that are frustrated with the economy, unemployment, illegals and wasteful spending.

God Bless our Military. How many of you civilians would be brave enough to give your life for the United States? Instead there are the whiners that do not understand what it is to be proud to be an American. They would rather be quite and not be disturbed. What they should be doing is saying thank you for making the United States a great place to live.

Luke Air Force Base is located west of Phoenix and is rapidly being surrounded by civilians that complain about the noise from the base and its planes, forgetting that it was there long before they were. A certain lieutenant colonel at Luke Air Force Base deserves a big pat on the back. Apparently, an individual who lives somewhere near Luke Air Force Base wrote the local paper complaining about a group of F-16's that disturbed their day at the mall.

When that individual read the response from a Luke Air Force Base Officer, it must have stung quite a bit.

The Complaint:

The question of the day for Luke Air Force Base?

Whom do we thank for the morning air show? Last Wednesday, at precisely 9:11 A.M, a tight formation of four F-16 jets made a low pass over Arrowhead Mall, continuing west over Bell Road at approximately 500 feet. Imagine our good fortune! Do the Tom Cruise-wannabes feel we need this wake-up call, or were they trying to impress the cashiers at Mervyns early bird special? Any response would be appreciated.

The Response:

Regarding the wake-up call from Luke's jets on June 15, at precisely 9:12 A.M. a perfectly timed four-ship fly by of F-16's from the 63rd Fighter Squadron at Luke Air Force Base flew over the grave of Capt. Jeremy Fresques. Capt Fresques was an Air Force Officer who was previously stationed at Luke Air Force Base and was killed in Iraq on May 30, Memorial Day.

At 9 A. M. on June 15, his family and friends gathered at Sunland Memorial Park in Sun City to mourn the loss of a husband, son and friend. Based on the letter writer's recount of the fly by, and because of the jet noise, I'm sure you didn't hear the 21-gun salute, the playing of taps, or my words to the widow and parents of Capt. Fresques as I gave them their son's flag on behalf of the President of the United States and all those veterans and servicemen and women who understand the sacrifices they have endured.

A four-ship fly by is a display of respect the Air Force gives to those who give their lives in defense of freedom. We are professional aviators and take our jobs seriously, and on June 15 what the letter writer witnessed was four officers lining up to pay their ultimate respects.

The letter writer asks, 'Whom do we thank for the morning air show? The 56th Fighter Wing will make the call for you, and forward your thanks to the widow and parents of Capt. Fresques, and thank them for you, for it was in their honor that my pilots flew the most honorable formation of their lives.

Only 2 defining forces have ever offered to die for you. Jesus Christ and the American Soldier.

One died for your soul, the other for your freedom.

Lt. Col. Grant L. Rosensteel, Jr.
United States Air Force

GOOD MORNING, WELCOME TO THE UNITED STATES OF AMERICA

Friends described one of the main reasons they moved from California. They bought their first home when they were in their very early twenty's in a middle class neighborhood in the high desert of California. Both of them had to commute 50 miles each way to be able to afford their home. It was 1400 a square foot single story with a small dirt yard, which they worked hard to turn into a nice, grass and tree filled place for their family to enjoy. Fast forward 8 years. Their neighbors decided to move and rent their 2300 square foot two story house with a nice big pool. They rented it Section 8. In moves a family of less fortunate. The renters were a mother, grandmother and 7 kids under high school age. The first thing that changed was the screens came off the upstairs windows above the garage so the kids sit on the roof an yell at other kids passing by. Then the garbage started piling up on the side of the house. The once nice yard grew and grew and grew. No lawn mower, thus no grass cutting. Looked like a vacant property sitting next to the lovely yard they worked so hard to keep nice (you know, to try to help keep up the neighborhood property values). The wonderful pool that we could only dream of having ourselves, turned green and soon had old plastic patio furniture and other discarded objects floating in it. Neither adult in the house had a job. Neither ever left the house except to go to the grocery store to use their assumed government food stamps and then return their plunder in a shopping carts which started to accumulate around the neighborhood. It didn't take long for others to join the Section 8 program and basically destroy our once nice, quite neighborhood. It was such a joy that we had to leave every morning for our long commute and jobs knowing that their neighborhood was in the able hands of the government blood suckers to continue their destruction. So these useless excuses for human beings who were less fortunate individuals were able to live hassle free in a house they could only dream about, while we had to pay for child care so we could both go to work. They sure appreciate the American dream of home ownership. They don't believe Democrat or Republican is so cut and dry, but they will never understand the thinking behind feeling sorry for people like this. It's time this country starts looking out for those who do something productive and pay taxes. We need to stop putting so much effort into making sure those who do not contribute to society are taken care of. Leave the assistance for those who truly need it because it's these abuses like above that has got people riled up. The Democrats would love to have people think it's not a problem, or that it's a small portion of the problem, but it's not. It's like a disease.

During the last days of the mid-term elections President Obama continued his campaigning gusto covering several states in pursuit of some Democratic votes. The President has attacked the Republican Party with causing the economic problems that the country is facing.

Harry Reid is a huge part of the Problem. The Democrats have nothing positive to say so they make personal attacks on the other candidates.

The Democrats can't campaign on passing obamacare because the people were against the program. They can't campaign on the deficit because they agreed with spending policies that have added $5 trillion to the deficit in the last three years. Then we have a Pelosi quote in 2007. "I swear it will pay as you go". They can't campaign on the financial reforms because they create permanent TARP. They can't campaign of stimulus because billions were wasted. They certainly can't campaign on jobs being created for the American workers.

The Democrats can't campaign on ethics and transparency. They can't campaign on Fannie Mae and Freddie Mac because the Democrats need the welfare vote even though it has ruined the housing markets. They can't campaign on racism as they play that card at the drop of a hat. They can't blame Bush anymore.

Then the President of the United States made personal attacks. They have nothing else to campaign on except trying to raise dirt about their opponent. When Obama made the comment that the Republicans should get to the back of the bus.

Obama is going to the United Nations. Whoopee! Now, he's going to make a fool of himself again, just as he did when he encouraged the United Nations to support his views on the Arizona SB-1070 law. Who is he after this time? North Carolina? Delaware? How about Minnesota? Along with his silly, over the hill bottle blond pal, Hillary, he will make grandiose promises, saying he has ended the war in Iraq, but won't give the credit to those who actually did the work, will expound grandly about his "push" in Afghanistan, but won't mention the fact that he won't allow our soldiers and Marines to fight, in fact, he wants them slaughtered, then he can disarm the nation entirely! He has already cut our nuclear weapons to the lowest number, and what he will do if we are attacked on his watch, he hasn't said, unless he's planning to bow to the invaders. He will also go into great details about his "war" on poverty, never mind the fact that he has put the majority of us in that category. As a president, this "man" is the biggest joke known to man. He is working very hard to take our Second Amendment Rights away, just as he has done with our First Amendment Rights, and fully intends to sell us out to the United Nations. In fact, watch for him to make a few advances along those lines while he's there. And, are the Democrats actually sure he is who he says he is? How do they know? Has anyone seen his actual birth certificate? Not just some piece of paper that could be bought in Hawaii.

Since 2007, the Democrats, Obama, Pelosi and Reid have added pork projects and used back door deals to get votes for their states destroying policies, enough of them, they have been in control too long and it was not good for this country. They throw lots of trash and smear and the Republicans, but they pretend they are squeaky clean, they should be investigated thoroughly and have their dirty laundry thrown out for all to see. Pelosi wants to take away from some people, why doesn't she start with herself, Reid and Obama?

Pelosi's comment, unemployment is good for the economy, what planet is she from or has she lost her brains with age. Time to get rid of these power grabbing fools and put new blood in that has a little more sense and hopefully will get the deficit down, bring jobs and bring the country back together, unlike this so called President that only kisses up to certain groups that he thinks can get votes from and throws the rest of the Americans under the bus. Did you ever see a President call half of America enemies, sue one of our own states, stick up for Muslims and throw the rest of the Religions in this country under the bus. Change our words to suit him, half the country protesting and hating each other, thanks to this idiot divider President.

If any of the groups of people that Obama is reaching out to for votes think he cares about them, they are sadly mistaking. He cares about no one but himself and his total power over this country.

Obama has done nothing but lie and take advantage of people who think the Democratic Party is the same as it has always been. It isn't. It was hijacked by a bunch of rich elite liberals who may have enough money to spread their wealth, but for those of us who work for a living we don't have it to spare. And if we do we would give it to our families first. I am a giving person, but I wish to pick who I give to and my family is first.

What an amazing country we have! Only in America could someone be elected President who was an illegal immigrant from Kenya, who never held a working job, who was elected a Senator and served just a short few months, whose biggest claim to fame is he was a community organizer, refuses to post his college scores (if he even and got a degree?) who refuses to produce his birth certificate, who doesn't even honor the flag or the national anthem, whose close friend was an avowed terrorist author, whose sat in church where the minister cursed the United States of America for years but never heard it, is a devout Muslim trying to hide and deny it, can't speak except to read a teleprompter, looks like a black Alfred E. Newman, (what me worry?) whose wife says she has never been proud of America, that she hates living like a fairy tale queen on the taxpayers dole, who takes numerous vacation and brings along all the people she has ever met in her life, who hates the free market, all white people, embraces socialism and calling it progressive, thinks if someone wants to kill you should just be tolerant, believes that the way to honor the 9/11 victims is to build a monument to the attackers. The list is so long that I give out trying to name them all and all of this is possible because his campaign made a majority of voters feel guilty for being white, and to punish their self and the country they elected the first token black president and called it the ultimate affirmative action. Now when it is almost too late they have arrived at their senses and want to make amends if it is at all now possible? Only in America remember that common sense can't be taught and stupid can't be cured.

Voting them out is not the only issue, nor is it just about being Republican or Democrat. All are being targeted if they keep doing the things that are destroying this nation. That is the whole reason the Tea Party movement sprang into being. The people have been silent and lazy for decades, letting the politicians ruin this country bit by bit. That seemed to give the green light to the progressives and they went full steam ahead. Now we see where we are; utterly destroyed as an economic power and worse. The country is being taken over by illegals with a wide open southern border which President Obama, won't stop from happening so Arizona has to make a law to do something about it, which Obama stops. Racism is more rampant now then when it was on its way to mending. Black Panther "kill all crackers and their cracker babies", is let loose when he clearly violated the law. Protecting Muslims and their victory mosque; snubbing the day of prayer and going to a mosque instead. The President showed disrespect for the leader of Israeli when he came to visit Washington. It will take a miracle to reverse this countries heading, and it will take a lot of giving up of things we do not need.

Since Nancy Pelosi assumed the House Speaker role, she has had a hand in adding $5 trillion to the nation's debt. She promised us fiscal discipline when signing onto the job. She also promised to drain the swamp and the swamp critters (Rangel, Waters & Frank) are still going strong. Now, thus far, no appropriations bills have been passed and claimed there was no better way to add jobs than to pass another unemployment benefit extension. We need to make judgments based on action, on the things that are done and not on the basis of what we are told. No Democrats are running on their record of passing Obamacare, the failed stimulus and its fake 3.3 million jobs saved or created or the finance law because the facts of what they have done will drive voters away. Bye Nancy - Supreme Queen of the swamp.

Foreigners gained 656,000 jobs in the first year following the official end of the recession in June 2009. American workers lost 1.2 million jobs, according to an analysis of government data by Pew, a nonpartisan research group.

As a result, the unemployment rate for immigrant workers fell to 8.7% from 9.3% between June 2009 and June 2010. For native-born workers, the rate rose to 9.7% from 9.2%. -- Wall Street Journal 2010

Is it possible that the electorate has finally figured out that rhetoric doesn't outweigh results? How about the non-issue mail you're receiving? Is most of it from the Democrats? I know that in this election I will be voting for all Republicans, not because I am a Republican, but because the Democrats have failed as a party. As far as I'm concerned we gave to much away in the last election, and I will not be as flexible with the Republicans when they get in, if they don't deliver, and quickly, I will be looking for similarly minded Americans to form a third party with a clearly defined platform for the people, and not the politicians. We need to take back this country, and we do not need a political aristocracy to do so.

Yes Carter and then Clinton took us down the road to no return and Obama is trying to finish us off. It is time to take our country back from this administration and demand that the Congressmen and Senators all read and understand what the bills they will vote on means and make sure they are for the Pledge of Allegiance to the flag and Constitution and the country before they take office. It is time that the will of the people will be voted and not shut down. It is time for the government of the people by the people and for the people to rise up and be seen and heard. Enough of the voting on what the Congressman or Senator thinks or some back door deals with some other party. Party time is over. They shall vote not what they think but what the constituency wants and demands. And guard the constitution as the protector of our lives which it is. Voting in a man is easy but voting in one who will do what the people want has become hard. This should be made a mandatory requirement to even hold the position as a representative. They have forgotten that representative means they are standing in for us and not themselves and what they want. It might bog congress down a little and appear they would get nothing done if they took the time to understand what it is they are doing but hey look what we got now and they are being paid a disgraceful salary and benefit package compared to the amount of work they actually do and then after they do it we get this?

I'm wondering how much it is costing the taxpayer to pay for Obama to fly around on his campaign effort. Shouldn't the bill go to the Democratic Party? I don't want my tax dollars that I worked hard to earn to be spent on a party I do not support.

On top of that the Democrats called Senator McCain every vile name they can possibly come up with. Then these groups and the Democratic National Convention sent teams of attorneys after Sarah Palin with drummed up ethics charges, non of which were ever upheld; then they attacked Joe the Plummer for asking a simple question and tried to literally ruin this man's life, as well as, dozens of other people;

And then Clinton and his Democrat progressive groups get upset about a couple of people with bull-horns interrupting their campaign speeches. Wow! These so called people are beyond extreme.

After decades of watching these tactics, I am so glad people are waking up and going to the polls to send the message; we are sick of the progressive movement, the Democrat Party and media lies. We are not putting up with it anymore.

O'Donnell dabbled in witchcraft in High School, Obama dabbled in cocaine. The ghostwriter for his book Bill Ayers dabbled in terrorism, Valerie Judd and Van Jones dabbled in communism. Tim Geithner dabbled in tax fraud. I could do this all day, we know more about O'Donnell then Obama.

Our traitorous President just turned his own country into the United Nations for Human Rights violations using Arizona as his example. Crying to what he considers Mommy. Already sees the United Nations as the Global Government. Search Google for the petition against it at the American Center for Law and Justice. The Democrats have to go.

President Obama's State Department has filed an unprecedented report with the United Nations Human Rights Council citing Arizona's immigration law as a human rights problem in this country. That's right the Obama Administration, which is challenging the Arizona law in federal court, is now appealing to the United Nations and to some of the most repressive countries in the world actually citing the Arizona law as an example of human rights abuses in this country.

Obama's agenda is still the same. To apologize for everything the United States does and to destroy the economy of the United States. To denigrate anything good the United States has done before his rule and to create a fascist socialist United States with a huge central government that "giveth and taketh away" at his personal whim.

I would guess most of the agenda will be apologizing for every thing we've ever done. The United Nations is not a viable global problem solver. It just seems a forum for anti Unites States rhetoric. If we pulled out it would implode. The United Nations troops aren't used when needed and corruption is the word of the day. Since we can not correct it we should abandon it.

Obama's agenda in six easy steps: 1. Spend ten times more money in a single year than your predecessor spent in 8 on kickbacks to your buddies. 2. Pass laws that hurt the people you are sworn to protect and only ensure higher rates of unemployment, higher taxes, and more bills for them to pay. 3. Blame any mishap on one of the industries that support you and on one owned by someone who does not agree with you, even if you have to warp the facts to do so. 4. Promise transparency and force a personal communication device that cannot be monitored into your possession so that you may make back-door deals. 5. Blame Bush for everything. 6. When number 5 doesn't work, blame the Republicans for everything and when they cry foul, watch as the left wing steps in and turn it into a bickering childish debate while you shove what you want through the back door.

Time for Obama to rally world support by reminding them that he is the one who hates America and is bringing it to it's knees, and to let them know that if he is not re-elected they might have to deal with a president who actually likes America and may not be willing to apologize for it the way he does.

As a recently retired school teacher of 36 years and a Union president for 12 of those, I firmly stand with the Republicans on this. The teachers unions are nothing more than blood suckers and I know the maority of teachers would NOT be in the union if it were not for the closed shop policy. THESE UNIONS WILL BE THE DEMISE OF THIS ONCE GRAT COUNTRY unless the Republicans can stop them

This is the only flag that every American should fly with pride and recite the Pledge of Allegiance to while holding their right hand over their heart.

CHAPTER TWELVE:

Who is President Obama?

My American Dream would be to have the President of the United States and all representatives of the Congress provide the information to the country to certify that they are qualified to hold their respective offices.

There has been an article on the You Tube that was released on October 25, 2010 that was written by Bob Unruh on October 2, 2010 stating that Barack H. Obama might not actually be Constitutionally Certified. There exists the possibility that the President is actually an illegal.

There has been a new petition filed with the 3rd United States Court of Appeals. The Democrats failed to certify that Barack H. Obama was Constitutional Certified to be the President of the United States.

What is really questionable to me is why would Barack Obama spend in excess of $1 million to have all his historical records purged or hidden from the people of the United States? He has made a statement that what does the American people want him to do "Wear a copy of his birth certificate on his forehead"? No we would just like your private documents made public and then have you Constitutionally Certified to hold the office of President.

President Obama has had every record purged from the public including his birth certificate, all his college transcripts, his passport information and his travel records abroad. All of these documents could establish the facts about his history. What does he have to hide? These are such simple request that a cave man could comply with them.

Barack Obama during his Cairo speech, said: "I know, too, that Islam has always been a part of America's story."

AN AMERICAN CITIZEN'S RESPONSE:

Dear Mr. Obama:

Were those the Muslims that were in America when the Pilgrims first landed? Funny, I thought they were Native American Indians.

Were those the Muslims that celebrated the first Thanksgiving Day? Sorry again, those were Pilgrims and Native American Indians.

Can you show me one Muslim signature on the United States Constitution? The Declaration of Independence? The Bill of Rights?

I didn't think so.

Did Muslims fight for this country's freedom from England? No.

Did Muslims fight during the Civil War to free the slaves in America? No, they did not. In fact, Muslims to this day are still the largest traffickers in human slavery. Your own half brother, a devout Muslim, still advocates slavery himself, even though Muslims of Arabic descent refer to black Muslims as "pug nosed slaves." Says a lot of what the Muslim world really thinks of your family's "rich Islamic heritage," doesn't it Mr. Obama?

Where were the Muslims during the Civil Rights era of this country? Not present.

There are no pictures or media accounts of Muslims walking side by side with Martin Luther King, Jr. or helping to advance the cause of Civil Rights.

Where were the Muslims during this country's Woman's Suffrage era? Again, not present. In fact, devout Muslims demand that women are subservient to men in the Islamic culture. So much so, that often they are beaten for not wearing the 'hajib' or for talking to a man who is not a direct family member or their husband. Yep, the Muslims are all for women's rights, aren't they?

Where were the Muslims during World War II? They were aligned with Adolf Hitler. The Muslim grand mufti himself met with Adolf Hitler, reviewed the troops and accepted support from the Nazi's in killing Jews.

Finally, Mr. Obama, where were Muslims on Sept. 11th, 2001? If they weren't flying planes into the World Trade Center, flying into the Pentagon or a field in Pennsylvania killing nearly 3,000 people on our own soil, they were rejoicing in the Middle East. No one can dispute the pictures shown from all parts of the Muslim world celebrating on CNN, Fox News, MSNBC and other cable news networks that day. Strangely, the very "moderate" Muslims who's asses you bent over backwards to kiss in Cairo, Egypt on June 4th were stone cold silent post 9-11. To many Americans, their silence has meant approval for the acts of that day.

And that, Mr. Obama, is the "rich heritage" Muslims have here in America.

Oh, I'm sorry I forgot to mention the Barbary Pirates. They were Muslim.

And now we can add November 5, 2009 - the slaughter of American soldiers at Fort Hood by a Muslim major who is a doctor and a psychiatrist who was supposed to be counseling soldiers returning from battle in Iraq and Afghanistan.

That, Mr. Obama is the "Muslim heritage" in America.

EVERY AMERICAN MUST READ THIS.

GOD BLESS AMERICA

The Fundamental Transformation of America

When Obama wrote a book and said he was mentored as a youth by Frank, (Frank Marshall Davis) an avowed Communist, people said it didn't matter.

When it was discovered that his grandparents, were strong socialists who sent Obama's mother to a socialist school where she was introduced to Frank Marshall Davis. He was later introduced to young Barrack Hussein Obama, people said it didn't matter.

When people found out that Barrack Hussein Obama was enrolled as a Muslim child in school and his father and stepfather were both Muslims, people said it didn't matter.

When he wrote in another book he authored "I will stand with them (Muslims) should the political winds shift in an ugly direction", people said it didn't matter.

When he admittedly, in his book, said he chose Marxist friends and professors in college, people said it didn't matter.

When he traveled to Pakistan, after college on an unknown national passport, people said it didn't matter.

When he sought the endorsement of the Marxist Party in 1996 as he ran for the Illinois Senate, people said it doesn't matter.

When he sat in a Chicago Church for twenty years and listened to a preacher spew hatred for America and preach black liberation theology, people said it didn't matter.

When an independent Washington organization, that tracks Senate voting records, gave him the distinctive title as the "most liberal senator," people said it didn't matter.

When the Palestinians in Gaza set up a fund raising telethon to raise money for his election campaign, people said it didn't matter.

When his voting record supported gun control, people said it didn't matter.

When he refused to disclose who donated money to his election campaign, as other candidates had done, people said it didn't matter.

When he received endorsements from people like Louis Farrakhan and Mummar Kadaffi and Hugo Chavez, people said it didn't matter.

When it was pointed out that he was a total newcomer and had absolutely no experience at anything except community organizing, people said it didn't matter.

When he chose friends and acquaintances such as Bill Ayers and Bernadine Dohrn who were revolutionary radicals, people said it didn't matter.

When his voting record in the Illinois senate and in the U.S. Senate came into question, people said it didn't matter.

When he refused to wear a flag, lapel pin, and did so only after a public outcry, people said it didn't matter.

When people started treating him as a Messiah and children in schools were taught to sing his praises, people said it didn't matter.

When he stood with his hands over his groin area for the playing of the National Anthem and Pledge of Allegiance, people said it didn't matter.

When he surrounded himself in the White House with advisors who were pro-gun control, pro-abortion, pro-homosexual marriage and wanting to curtail freedom of speech to silence the opposition, people said it didn't matter.

When he said he favors sex education in Kindergarten, including homosexual indoctrination, people said it didn't matter.

Well, for all of the people that said it didn't matter I hope you are satisfied with what you have received with your choice of President of the United States of America.

One thing is very important. The majority of Americans think these things do matter and our President has not lived up to the qualifications of the office of the President.

CHAPTER THIRTEEN:

Democratic Scams at Voting Polls

Some voters in Boulder City, Nevada complained that their ballot had been cast before they went to the polls, raising questions about Clark County's electronic voting machines. The voters said when they went to vote for Republican Democratic opponent's name was already checked.

The voter said they weren't alone in her voting experience. She said her husband and several others voting at the same time all had the same thing happen. "Something's not right," the voter said. "One person that's could be an accident. Two would be strange. But several within a five minute period of time that means something is definitely wrong."

An aide to Senate Majority Leader Harry Reid repeatedly lied to federal immigration and FBI agents and submitted false federal documents to the Department of Homeland Security to cover up her illegal seven-year marriage to a Lebanese national who was the subject of an Oklahoma City Joint Terror Task Force investigation. Reid's Hispanic Press Secretary, admitted to receiving payment for some of her expenses in exchange for fraudulently marrying Bassam Mahmoud Tarhini in 2003, strictly so he could obtain permanent United States residency.

The aide to Senator Reid was never charged. Isn't that kind of ironic since every other woman that participated in a fraudulent marriage to evade immigration laws which is a Class D Felony would be prosecuted? The prosecutor stated "We did not charge the woman, and of course we don't discuss the reasons we don't charge people." Could there have been some extreme pressure from Senator Reid?

The same aide to Senator Reid was still appearing as a guest on a Spanish-language radio program in her official capacity as a spokeswoman for Senator Reid.

The highest level of management inside the Department of Homeland Security was aware that she worked for Reid, multiple sources confirmed, and following protocol, the majority leader should have been informed of the investigation through those channels, as well.

CHAPTER FOURTEEN:

The Federal Reserve

We are going to try and figure out why the Federal Reserve is holding the interest rates they are charging the banks to borrow money at close to zero. I have never understood why the Federal Reserve thinks that providing the massive amount of funds to the likes of Bank of America, Chase Manhattan, Wells Fargo and many other banks is going to help the economy. The theory of the program is to provide more capital that the banks can lend to the businesses and middle class Americans. That is really the stupidest program that has ever been designed. All this does is let the banks have huge amounts of capital that they don't have to pay interest on so they can turn around and loan it to the American citizens at any where from 5% to 18% that they charge the consumer. The only one that wins in this situation is the banks. No wonder their financial statements are looking better. If I could borrow $1 billion and earn an average of 10% on the money my financial statements would look much better too. The Federal Reserve is just pumping profits into the banks instead of helping the citizens of the United States. What will eventually happen is that the United States is going to fall into a deeper recession than we are already in.

The American citizens and small businesses are not going to borrow money they do not have any way of repaying. It is too bad that the federal government can not operate on the same principles. The businesses are not going to borrow money unless there are ways they can earn profits from the loan that exceed the costs to borrow. Businesses are not going to hire more employees until these employees can produce enough products or services to pay for the cost to the employer. Borrowing money is not the answer since it eventually has to be repaid. That does not improve the economy. Then we have the banks creating excessive lending requirements so that the majority of the applicants do not qualify. This will keep the funds available for the banks use instead of stimulating the economy.

The Federal Reserve is pumping all this money into the large banks so that they can pump the money into the economy but instead of loaning the money they are investing in the stock market and other high risk commodity futures. With all the buying pressure they are putting on the market it will continue to improve in the short term. The day is going to arrive fairly soon when all these bank investments are going to need to be sold and they are hoping that the small investors will be suckered back into the raising market so they can liquidate their holdings. Again the little guy gets screwed and the big banks reap their huge profits at the expense of the citizens.

The Federal Reserve is not willing to accept the fact that their programs is doomed to fail. It is like most of the programs that the current administration is promoting. The common sense is that by keeping the interest rates at these low levels is that they are killing the 58 million senior citizens that rely on receiving interest on their savings accounts and because of the Federal Reserve policy have been reduced to a 1% return. This cuts into the amount of income the seniors have to spend and further stifles the economic growth of the country.

A BRIEF HISTORY OF THE FEDERAL RESERVE

The conspiracy to form the Federal Reserve System was carried out during the night of November 22, 1910. A delegation of the nation's leading financiers left the train station in Hoboken, New Jersey on a very secret mission. It would be years before anyone found out what the mission was. Even then they would not understand that the history of the United States underwent a drastic change after that night in Hoboken.

The delegation traveled in a sealed railway car for Jekyll Island. The group was led by Senator Nelson Aldrich, head of the National Monetary Commission. President Theodore Roosevelt had signed into law the bill creating the National Monetary Commission in 1908, after the tragic Panic of 1907 had resulted in a public outcry that the nation's monetary system be stabilized. Aldrich had led the members of the Commission on a two-year tour of Europe, spending some three hundred thousand dollars of public money. He had not yet made a report on the results of this trip, nor had he offered any plan for banking reform.

Accompanying Senator Aldrich at the Hoboken station were his private secretary, Shelton; A. Piatt Andrew, Assistant Secretary of the Treasury, and Special Assistant of the National Monetary Commission; Frank Vanderlip, president of the National City Bank of New York, Henry P. Davison, senior partner of J.P. Morgan Company, and generally regarded as Morgan's personal emissary; and Charles D. Norton, president of the Morgan-dominated First National Bank of New York. Joining the group just before the train left the station were Benjamin Strong, also known as a lieutenant of J.P. Morgan; and Paul Warburg, a recent immigrant from Germany who had joined the banking house of Kuhn, Loeb

These facts can be verified from information on the Internet. Thank God for today's modern technology. If you want to know where ot find the information send me an email. meinders@aol.com

"The Federal Reserve System was established by an act of Congress in 1913 and is not a 'private corporation'." On the next page, Mr. Winn continues, "The stock of the Federal Reserve Banks is held entirely by commercial banks that are members of the Federal Reserve System." He offers no explanation as to why the government has never owned a single share of stock in any Federal Reserve Bank, or why the Federal Reserve System is not a "private corporation" when all of its stock is owned by "private corporations".

The main problem, as Paul Warburg informed his colleagues, was to avoid the name "Central Bank". For that reason, he had decided upon the designation of "Federal Reserve System". This would deceive the people into thinking it was not a central bank. However, the Jekyll Island plan would be a central bank plan, fulfilling the main functions of a central bank; it would be owned by private individuals who would profit from ownership of shares. As a bank of issue, it would control the nation's money and credit.

Thus the proposed Federal Reserve Bank was to be "controlled by Congress" and answerable to the government, but the majority of the directors were to be chosen, "directly or indirectly" by the banks of the association. In the final refinement of Warburg's plan, the Federal Reserve Board of Governors would be appointed by the President of the United States, but the real work of the Board would be controlled by a Federal Advisory Council, meeting with the Governors. The Council would be chosen by the directors of the twelve Federal Reserve Banks, and would remain unknown to the public.

Warburg responded that the administrators of the proposed central banks should be subject to executive approval by the President. This patent removal of the system from Congressional control meant that the Federal Reserve proposal was unconstitutional from its inception, because the Federal Reserve System was to be a bank of issue. Article 1, Sec. 8, Par. 5 of the Constitution expressly charges Congress with "the power to coin money and regulate the value thereof.". Warburg's plan would deprive Congress of its sovereignty, and the systems of checks and balances of power set up by Thomas Jefferson in the Constitution would now be destroyed. Administrators of the proposed system would control the nation's money and credit, and would themselves be approved by the executive department of the government. The judicial department (the Supreme Court, etc.) was already virtually controlled by the executive department through presidential appointment to the bench.

Another member of the "First Name Club" was less reticent. Frank Vanderlip later published a few brief references to the conference. In the Saturday Evening Post, February 9, 1935, Vanderlip wrote: "Despite my views about the value to society of greater publicity for the affairs of corporations, there was an occasion near the close of 1910, when I was as secretive, indeed, as furtive, as any conspirator. . . . Since it would have been fatal to Senator Aldrich's plan to have it known that he was calling on anybody from Wall Street to help him in preparing his bill, precautions were taken that would have delighted the heart of James Stillman (a colorful and secretive banker who was President of the National City Bank during the Spanish-American War, and who was thought to have been involved in getting us into that war). I do not feel it is any exaggeration to speak of our secret expedition to Jekyll Island as the occasion of the actual conception of what eventually became the Federal Reserve System."

Edward Vreeland, co-author of the bill, wrote in the August 25, 1910 Independent (which was owned by Aldrich), "Under the proposed monetary plan of Senator Aldrich, monopolies will disappear, because they will not be able to make more than four percent interest and monopolies cannot continue at such a low rate. Also, this will mark the disappearance of the Government from the banking business."

Vreeland's fantastic claims were typical of the propaganda flood unleashed to pass the Aldrich Plan. Monopolies would disappear, the Government would disappear from the banking business. Pie in the sky.

Nation Magazine, January 19, 1911, noted, "The name of Central Bank is carefully avoided, but the 'Federal Reserve Association', the name given to the proposed central organization, is endowed with the usual powers and responsibilities of a European Central Bank."

CHAIRMAN CARTER GLASS: "Why didn't the Western bankers make themselves heard when the American Bankers Association gave its unqualified and, we are assured, unanimous approval of the scheme proposed by the National Monetary Commission?"

ANDREW FRAME: "I'm glad you called my attention to that. When that monetary bill was given to the country, it was but a few days previous to the meeting of the American Bankers Association in New Orleans in 1911. There was not one banker in a hundred who had read that bill. We had twelve addresses in favor of it. General Hamby of Austin, Texas, wrote a letter to President Watts asking for a hearing against the bill. He did not get a very courteous answer. I refused to vote on it, and a great many other bankers did likewise."

MR. BULKLEY: "Do you mean that no member of the Association could be heard in opposition to the bill?"

ANDREW FRAME: "They throttled all argument."

MR. KINDRED: "But the report was given out that it was practically unanimous."

ANDREW FRAME: "The bill had already been prepared by Senator Aldrich and presented to the executive council of the American Bankers Association in May, 1911. As a member of that council, I received a copy the day before they acted upon it. When the bill came in at New Orleans, the bankers of the United States had not read it."

MR. KINDRED: "Did the presiding officer simply rule out those who wanted to discuss it negatively?"

ANDREW FRAME: "They would not allow anyone on the program who was not in favor of the bill."

CHAIRMAN GLASS: "What significance has the fact that at the next annual meeting of the American Bankers Association held at Detroit in 1912, the Association did not reiterate its endorsement of the plan of the National Monetary Commission, known as the Aldrich scheme?"

ANDREW FRAME: "It did not reiterate the endorsement for the simple fact that the backers of the Aldrich Plan knew that the Association would not endorse it. We were ready for them, but they did not bring it up."

We object to the Aldrich Bill on the following points: Its entire lack of adequate government or public control of the banking mechanism it sets up. It's tendency to throw voting control into the hands of the large banks of the system. The extreme danger of inflation of currency is inherent in the system.

The insincerity of the bond-funding plan provided for by the measure, there being a barefaced pretense that this system was to cost the government nothing. The dangerous monopolistic aspects of the bill.

"Our financial system is a false one and a huge burden on the people . . . This Act establishes the most gigantic trust on earth."--Congressman Charles Augustus Lindbergh, Sr.

Senator LaFollette publicly charged that a money trust of fifty men controlled the United States. George F. Baker, partner of J.P. Morgan, on being queried by reporters as to the truth of the charge, replied that it was absolutely in error. He said that he knew from personal knowledge that not more than eight men ran this country.

The Presidential campaign of 1912 records one of the more interesting political upsets in American history. The incumbent, William Howard Taft, was a popular president, and the Republicans, in a period of general prosperity, were firmly in control of the government through a Republican majority in both houses. The Democratic challenger, Woodrow Wilson, Governor of New Jersey, had no national recognition, and was a stiff, austere man who excited little public support. Both parties included a monetary reform bill in their platforms: The Republicans were committed to the Aldrich Plan, which had been denounced as a Wall Street plan, and the Democrats had the Federal Reserve Act. Neither party bothered to inform the public that the bills were almost identical except for the names. In retrospect, it seems obvious that the money creators decided to dump Taft and go with Wilson. How do we know this? Taft seemed certain of re-election and Wilson would return to obscurity. Suddenly, Theodore Roosevelt "threw his hat into the ring." He announced that he was running as a third party candidate, the "Bull Moose". His candidacy would have been ludicrous had it not been for the fact that he was exceptionally well-financed. Moreover, he was given unlimited press coverage, more than Taft and Wilson combined. As a Republican ex-president, it was obvious that Roosevelt would cut deeply into Taft's vote. This proved the case, and Wilson won the election. To this day, no one can say what Theodore Roosevelt's program was, or why he would sabotage his own party. Since the bankers were financing all three candidates, they would win regardless of the outcome. Later Congressional testimony showed that in the firm of Kuhn Loeb Company, Felix Warburg was supporting Taft, Paul Warburg and Jacob Schiff was supporting Wilson, and Otto Kahn was supporting Roosevelt. The result was that a Democratic Congress and a Democratic President were elected in 1912 to get the central bank legislation passed. It seems probable that the identification of the Aldrich Plan as a Wall Street operation predicted that it would have a difficult passage through Congress, as the Democrats would solidly oppose it, whereas a successful Democratic candidate, supported by a Democratic Congress, would be able to pass the central bank plan. Taft was thrown overboard because the bankers doubted he could deliver on the Aldrich Plan and Roosevelt was the instrument of his demise. *The final electoral vote in 1912 was Wilson - 409; Roosevelt - 167; and Taft - 15.

Glass claimed that the proposed Federal Advisory Council would force the Federal Reserve Board of Governors to act in the best interest of the people.

Under the Federal Reserve Act, note circulation would always expand indefinitely, causing great inflation. However, the later history of the Federal Reserve System showed that it not only caused inflation, but that the issue of notes could also be restricted, causing deflation, as occurred from 1929 to 1939.

The Federal Reserve Act puts it in twelve regional central banks, all owned exclusively by the identical private interests that would have owned and operated the Aldrich Bank. President Garfield shortly before his assassination declared that whoever controls the supply of currency would control the business and activities of the people. Thomas Jefferson warned us a hundred years ago that a private central bank issuing the public currency was a greater menace to the liberties of the people than a standing army."

<u>The real question is who actually owns the Federal Reserve System today?</u>

As astonishing as it may sound the practice of passing legislation without reading it has been going on for over 100 years. The Healthcare bill was passed using these same tactics of voting without reading the bill. You would think that after 110 years that this country would have learned something.

Make sure every one of your representatives are sent a copy of this information.

GOD BLESS AMERICA

Nothing has ever been free for the freedom that we enjoy as Americans. God Bless America and the military personnel that keep us free.

CHAPTER FIFTEEN:

The National Debt

My American Dream would to be that the federal government would be required to submit proposals for a balanced budget every year. This great country can not keep adding to the deficit and leave such a mess for our children and grand children. At the current pace they will never get it paid in full.

The current administration, led by President Obama tries to sell the United States on the theory that deficit spending will cure the economic problems. Just how does he ever plan on paying this deficit off? Look out America, this President thinks raising taxes in going to be the answer.

Obama lacerates over exploding deficits? Since the Democrats have controlled both houses (including the last two years of Bush's term) the deficit has totally exploded. Don't blame the people who were not in power. If Congress did not want deficits then it would have done something with their spending habits.

We are going to discuss Mr. Obama's "Hope and Change" and get into some of the very biased reporting by the mainstream media outlets. When Obama first touted "Hope and Change" it was thought by most Americans that there would be the hope that government legislation would be for the people of the United States and that the change would

be for less government spending and a more stable economy. Here is what Obama meant by Hope. Hope we can cram enough spending bills down the taxpayer's throats while we have total control of the House of Representatives and Congress. We are going to spend more money than this country ever imagined while we can. By change, Obama meant that we were going to do everything we can to change the United States into a socialist country. We are going to change the way government is run. We don't care what the majority of the people want we are going to change it to my way or the highway. We don't know about what you are thinking but we believe that the government should be "We the People, By the People and For the People".

On September 18, 2010 there was an article posted by Yahoo that appeared to be from Time magazine. The headline was "Obama Gains Momentum in the Fight over Tax-Cut Extensions". This article was so biased in an attempt to sway the voters over what terrible people the Republicans are for holding the middle class hostage on the vote to extend the Bush tax cuts. The entire article aimed at portraying how evil the Republicans for not immediately voting to penalize the upper 2% of the taxpayers. Obama wants to give the so called middle class the tax cuts totaling $3.2 billion and wants the people that are paying over 50% of the taxes in the United States to be excluded from the tax reductions because it will add $700 million to the deficit. Where did Obama learn anything about business or the economy? These numbers were projected to be the costs over the next 10 years to the government. How about Obama getting serious about the real problem? First, taxes are paid to the government as a result of the hard work of the citizens. If the 2% of the working class is making more money then it is because they are working harder and smarter than the rest. They do not add to the deficit because the government has not earned the money yet. The deficit is created by the excess spending of the government. Saying that it cost the United States government $3.9 billion dollars is like saying we should be paid $100,000 a year and you are costing us $100,000 by not paying us and that was money that we are going to spend. Second, the total figure breaks down to $390 billion per year for the 10 year period. Obama and the Democrats passed legislation for a stimulus bill that cost $787 billion in the current year. These kind of spending policies by the government are what cause the deficit. Third, the article never mentioned the fact that over 30 Democrats are jumping ship and leaning towards the complete tax cut for every taxpayer. Now that is the momentum we need.

The Democrats are pushing for passage of the "National Defense Authorization Bill" by this week which has been scheduled by the Senate. To show the people just how underhanded the Democrats are they have included a portion that will end up giving amnesty to approximately 800,000 illegals. Instead of trying to pass the "Dream Act" that is being promoted by Reid as a stand alone bill they try to sneak it in on another. The public knows that the "Dream Act" that is proposed by Reid would never pass on the merits of that bill. Why not slam it home on something else? Maybe the public won't notice. That is really a good form of transparency, isn't it? Senator McCain is planning to filibuster and will only need 41 votes to stop this legislation. Hopefully the Senate will adjourn before anything can be passed.

Reid has gotten support for this from one very great political brain in the form of Lady Gaga. Now that is really getting support from one of the real intelligent people of the world. Reid supposedly tweeted Lady Gaga that this was an important vote before the mid-term election recess. Not only is that but Lady Gaga bad mouthing Senator McCain. Reid knows that if it can not be passed before the mid-term elections that it will never get passed. These two bills have absolutely nothing in common and never should be allowed to be voted on together. Again the Democrats are employing crooked politics.

There was an article that reported how the Hispanic voters placed their votes during the last 5 elections. This article was in the Newsweek magazine dated September 20, 2010. Over the last 5 elections the Hispanic voters were 62.4% in favor of the Democrats. Is it any wonder that Reid would like to give amnesty to the 800,000 Mexicans? During the last two elections the vote was 68% for the Democrats.

When Obama was campaigning he promised immigration reform. From what has transpired his type of reform was to sue the State of Arizona for enforcing the laws that are in effect. The Obama administration would like to give amnesty to the illegals that are in the United States. That could provide somewhere around 20,000,000 voters that have a history of voting Democratic. This administration is bound and determined to create a class division in the United States. What about everyone being Americans and not segregated by class? While we are on the subject there is no such thing as Mexican Americans. There are only Americans that support this country and what it stands for.

What is amazing is the Democratic Party has allowed candidates that are under ethics violations to continue to run for office. It must be that these candidates are in districts that continually vote Democratic regardless of what these incumbents have done? Let the sheep follow their leader and when they are convicted of ethics violations they will be able to appoint someone that will be one of their lemmings and vote exactly as our leader dictates. Now that is not the kind of government that most of the American voters want.

GOD BLESS AMERICA

CHAPTER SIXTEEN:

Illegals in America

Theodore Roosevelt's ideas on immigrants and being an American in 1907.

"In the first place, we should insist that if the immigrant who comes here in good faith becomes an American and assimilates himself to us, he shall be treated on an exact equality with everyone else, for it is an outrage to discriminate against any such man because of creed, or birthplace, or origin. But this is predicated upon the person's becoming in every facet an American and nothing but an American. There can be no divided allegiance here. Any man who says he is an American, but something else also, isn't an American at all. We have room for but one flag, the American flag... We have room for but one language here, and that is the English language... and we have room for but one sole loyalty and that is a loyalty to the American people."

Theodore Roosevelt 1907

It is about time we beefed up the borders and deported ALL illegal persons. If they want to come to America that is great, glad to have them. Just do it the legal way and come here correctly not as criminals.

An immigrant rights group has released a report predicting that 25 states may try next year to pass illegal immigration laws similar to Arizona's SB-1070 controversial legislation.

The new efforts are going forward even after a federal judge ruled key parts of the Arizona law unconstitutional and enjoined its enforcement in Arizona in July. That decision is now under appeal before the Ninth U.S. Circuit Court.

Georgia, Mississippi, Oklahoma and South Carolina are most likely to pass a similar law next year, the new report says. Tennessee, Utah, Florida, Nebraska, Pennsylvania, Texas, Arkansas, Indiana, Colorado, Virginia, Minnesota, Missouri, Idaho and Kansas made the report's "maybe" list. In Maryland, Nevada, Massachusetts, North Carolina, Michigan, Ohio and Rhode Island, the legislation is seen as less likely to pass.

This next wave of legislation will be aimed at getting local law enforcement to check immigration status in routine police stops, as SB-1070 mandates.

One industry stands to benefit from such laws. In Arizona's case, the private prison industry helped guide the process that made SB-1070 law and even gave the legislation its name while working with legislators,. Thirty of the cosponsors to SB-1070 later received money from the private prison industry or its lobbyists.

The Mexican government is concerned that the Arizona immigration law could affect relations with the State of Arizona.

The Mexican government has criticized a tough immigration law approved this by Arizona legislators, saying it could result in rights violations and racial profiling and affect cross border relations.

Mexico's Foreign Relations Department said in a statement relayed through Mexico's United States embassy that it viewed the measure with great concern and said it "could have potentially serious effects on the civil rights" of Mexican nationals.

"Mexico views with concern the possible negative effects the measure could have, if approved, on the development of the ties of friendship, culture, commerce and tourism that have characterized Mexico's relations with Arizona for generations," according to the statement. The law has been approved by the Arizona legislators and is awaiting consideration by Gov. Jan Brewer. The measures make it a state crime for migrants to be in Arizona without documents.

Mexico also said the bill "opens the door to the inappropriate use of racial profiling."

An estimated 20 million Mexicans live in the United States that are not documented, and Arizona has been one of the main routes for illegals to enter the United States.

We need to take care of America and not be concerned what the Mexican government thinks about our border security. When the 20 million illegals start going back to Mexico they will be singing a different tune while their country goes broke and not the United States going broke because of the illegals

The Federal Government of the United States has no right to sue any of the States over making laws on immigration according to Article 1 Section 8 Paragraph 4, Article 1 Section 9 Paragraphs 1 and 2; these references don't give the Feds supremacy rights over the States. Rule is not law, but law is rule, where as rule is a guide line to make law, making law governs behavior and is reserved to the States in Article 1 Section 9 Paragraphs 1 and 2. Article 1 Section 10 Paragraph 3 gives the rights to a State to declare war on a Foreign Power or Government if the Congress doesn't act. Article 1 Section 10 Paragraph 1 states that no State shall make letters of Marque and Reprisal with any Foreign Power or Government, therefore, A State can not issue an apology for the laws that may be offensive to another Country, nor, should a Foreign Country be allowed to issue statements, comments or letters of Marque and Reprisal to a State. Mexico is not responsible to control both sides of the border with any of the States of America, nor, is America responsible to control both sides of the borders of any States bordering with Mexico.

Mexico doesn't decide American law; neither does America decide law for Mexico. Nobody is reading the Constitution of the United States that way and with the intent in which it was written. The Federal government can't over rule on a supremacy clause do to Article 1 Section 8 Paragraph 4, Article 1 Section 9 Paragraphs 1 and 2 or Article 1 Section 10 paragraph 3, nor can the Fed force a State to make concessions with a Foreign Government under Article 1 Section 10 Paragraph 1, for offending a Foreign Government by the laws of the State.

America is not any different than Mexico on this issue. It is illegal to enter Mexico without the proper documents and they will, without question, hold you to their law and give you a hassle over their law prevails over American law, simply because you are in Mexico. So, where is the Racial Profiling, Hate, and Discrimination when America does the same thing to protect its side of the border? Americans don't, as norm, enter Mexico thru other than authorized point of entry, so there isn't a problem with Americans going to Mexico, but there is a problem with people crossing into America thru means other than authorized points of entry and trying to use American law as their right to do as they please. Nothing more could be wrongfully interpreted of the American law or Constitution.

This is what America really wants. Politicians will tell you there is no way out of this invasion...they are here, the horse is out of the barn, there is nothing we can do to deport them, etc. This is what they want us to think...the truth is there will be voluntary attrition through enforcement of law. This is exactly what happened in Arizona. They all started to pack up and leave for states that have a more welcome reception for them like California. If all of the 25 states mentioned above take the same stance, then they will forced to migrate to places like California since they will not enforce laws. Then it will be their problem to deal with. California is already bankrupt in large part because of the projected 10.8 million illegals already there.

There is a billboard close to the Arizona border that says it all about the feelings of the Arizona citizens.

"Attention Illegal Immigrants"

Arizona does not welcome you, but Los Angeles loves you.

Free Housing, Free School, Free Food, Free Medical, and Free Hospital.

No Insurance Costs, no taxes, and plenty of jobs.

TURN LEFT ON I-8 AND FOLLOW YOUR ROAD TO PARADISE!

It is good to see other states trying to do what's necessary to rid the country of the problem of illegals. This country can barely take care of its citizens, but the illegals and their supporters expect us to take care of illegals? This country is already in enough debt as it is. Yes it sounds harsh to deport illegals, but they've come over here, not caring about the law. They take jobs that could've gone to the citizens of the United States. There are lazy people in the United States for sure, but there are also many that would love to take over the jobs that illegals occupy. Many of them commit crimes. They crowd schools and cost hospitals a lot of money. They give nothing back, but expect more and then send billions of dollars back to Mexico. They have absolutely no loyalty to the United States.

For the record, I'm not against immigration from any race, as long as it's legal. I'm not against any race; I know there are smart, hard-working, respectful people from any race, just as there are stupid, lazy, inconsiderate ones from each race. Illegals whether they're from Mexico, Canada, Asia, Europe, anywhere, don't belong here. If they want to do things the right way, that's perfectly fine. But illegal intruders are not welcome here.

28% of California citizens are illegals. That is roughly 10.8 million people. California is way past broke and its infrastructure is crumbling under the weight of providing welfare, schools, roads, power, clean water, food, etc., for a flood of people that frankly don't belong there. If people immigrate legally, fine, as long as the numbers aren't too great. On the other hand if people flood across the borders by the tens of millions, our country will have no future for today's population or tomorrows. It's not racism or any other idiotic slur word. The right to safeguarding our country so your kids can have a future should be the first priority of our federal government.

The rest of the states need to join the 25 that are considering legislation similar to Arizona's SB-1070. This would be great for millions of Americans could get their jobs back from the illegals. It is hard for this country to run, when the people that have been paying taxes are losing there jobs and the ones that are not paying taxes are working and they are felons for being illegal. Maybe we should start taking actions like other countries do for illegals. There is a reason why they do it. Their policies protect the sovereign rights of their countries.

Here are some of the other countries immigration laws. If you cross the North Korean border illegally you get 12 years at hard labor. If you cross the Iranian border illegally you are detained indefinitely and Carter will beg for your release. If you cross the Afghan border illegally, you get shot. If you cross the Saudi Arabian border illegally you will be jailed. If you cross the Chinese border illegally you may never be heard from again. If you cross the Venezuelan border illegally you will be branded a spy and your fate will be sealed. If you cross the Mexican border illegally you will be jailed for two years. If you cross the Cuban border illegally you will be thrown into political prison to rot. If you cross the United States border illegally you get the following benefits

1 - A job. 2 - A driver's license. 3 - A Social Security card. 4 – Welfare. 5 - Food stamps. 6 – A lobbyist in Washington. 7 - Subsidized rent or a loan to buy a house. 8 – Credit cards. 9 - Free health care system. 10 – Free public education. 11 - Billions of dollars in public documents printed in your language. 12 - And the right to carry the flag of your country - the one you walked out on - while you call America racist and protest that you don't get enough respect. 13 - Country's laws do not apply to you.

Is it any wonder that the United States has a major problem with illegals entering into our country? Why doesn't our government do something about stopping the problem and deporting every illegal that is in the United States?

"Immigrant Rights Group"? I know a friend who legally came in from Britain and had some issues with the State Department. He went to an immigrant right group and got no help. As it turned out, these immigrant right groups have no interest in helping legal immigrants just the illegal ones. "We work for America" with a Mexican flag in the background.

Foreigners want to change our laws, make new laws and change our nation while still remaining proud citizens of Republic of Mexico.

First of all I refuse to call these people immigrants. They are illegals. There are plenty of applicants for legal immigration which in some instances can take more than 10 years. We need to reduce the magnet that draws these illegals. Write your Senator and Congressman to repeal the law that makes any individual born in the United States a citizen. The laws need to be changed to if an individual is born in the United States they will be a citizen if the mother was here legally and is in legal status, i.e., has not overstayed the visa.

Once we reduce the magnet that draws many, they will stop invading the United States. Yes I used the word invasion. An invasion that should be repelled by the military by any means necessary. Once people hear those sneaking across the border are subject to be shot, many will stop coming.

All employers must be able to prove due diligence when hiring an employee and if they can not they are severely fined. English needs again to become the national language and all people here need to learn the national language.

As a country we have become impenitent and we are giving the United States away and if not stopped immediately we will be destroyed.

If the Federal Government can not get this right and continue to do nothing, we must impeach all in office for treason.

If you want migrant workers then implement a migrant worker plan with annual permits. The employers that need migrant workers should be required to pay a fee to administer this program. When the seasonal work is done then the migrant workers need to return to the country that they came from. No exceptions.

Almost 2 million jobs have moved to immigrants from United States born workers since the most recent recession officially ended in June 2009 according to a current poll. Of course the American citizen does not think the recession has ended. It is just President Obama's lemmings that are trying to get America feel better about being unemployed.

United States born workers have lost about 1.2 million jobs since the recession officially ended in June 2009, while foreign-born workers gained 656,000 jobs. As a result, the unemployment rate for foreign-born workers, which was about even with their native United States counterparts during the recession, is now 8.7%, or about one percentage point less than United States born workers. This situation has to be corrected by the proper legislation in Washington.

Deport all the illegals and their anchor babies. Illegals account for 16% of the United States labor force, up from about 10% in 1995. Does anyone understand why our unemployment rate is so high? Eliminate all the illegals from the workforce and the unemployment rate will decline to the 4.5% range.

The Mexican government is going to be unhappy since the United States has confiscated 20 tons of pot near an underground tunnel in the United States. This will mean that about $25 million of American money will not be ending up in Mexico. The Mexican authorities did recover about 4 tons of pot on their side of the tunnel.

The United States authorities found the opening to the tunnel, which ran the length of six football fields under the border and ended at a warehouse in Mexico, The tunnel had lighting, ventilation and a rail system to send loads of illegal drugs into California.

United States officials have found 125 cross-border tunnels built by Mexican drug cartels to elude detection since the early 1990s. 75 of the tunnels have been found in the past four years. Many were discovered before they were completed. The majority were found along the California and Arizona borders with Mexico.

Both Governments say the drug war has not crossed over into America. It is time for some heavy duty bomb drops along the border to ruin these tunnels. More proof that America needs to completely shut down the border. Get the fence completed along with the America's Highway. Make it so the border crossings are the only way into the United States. No one comes into our country without a passport. Deport those illegals that are already here. That means all of them including their babies, mothers, fathers and spouses. Americans are sick of the illegals our country.

The War on Marijuana has be going on now for over 70 years. Presently the usage of marijuana is about the same as cigarettes among teenagers. Is that called success? Results are what matter. In the Netherlands, where it's legal, they have a far lower use of marijuana among teenagers. They have a sensible approach that works. Is marijuana a grave danger to society? Every year there is several hundred overdose deaths from alcohol. How many people died overdosing on marijuana? Zero. Alcohol is known to cause violent or aggressive behavior, marijuana does not. Some people think marijuana is the gateway drug to harder drugs. Why, because it's easier for a kid to buy marijuana than alcohol or cigarettes? Don't believe it? Do you think a drug dealer going to ask a kid for ID? What do you think would work best to reduce usage, changing people's mindset to live a healthy lifestyle, or the threat of going to prison? The tax monies would be better spent on education and PR campaigns. We must ask why our government is intentionally ignoring the facts. Currently the only thing wasted is tax money. Just look at the results, far more people have smoked marijuana today, by percentage, than in 1937. Our country's marijuana policy has been a failure from start to finish, and we've spent a lot of money going backwards. Also we lost all the tax monies by not taxing it. Talk about waste in government. Should the police and the courts continue to waste their resources on simple pot possession and use charges, while putting aside efforts on more serious crimes? The fact is prohibition gave rise to the power of organize crime. It is well known that Al Capone was a big supporter of the prohibition of alcohol. Why? There's a lot more profit to make in the untaxed market. There's so much profit that Capone bribed numerous politicians and law enforcement officials. When the prohibition of alcohol was lifted, the murder rate actually dropped. It brought the end of organized crime fighting for control of the alcohol market. Don't believe it? Is the cartels still smuggling alcohol over the border? No, that stopped with the end of prohibition of alcohol. That's called success! The strategy right now is to ensure that marijuana is not taxed or sales regulated. Presently the drug cartels are controlling the production and sale of marijuana, not our government. There is a drug war happening south of the border that is undermining the Mexican government. Half the revenue of the drug cartels comes from the production and sale of marijuana. By legalizing marijuana would effectively remove 50 percent of the cartels monies. And any business, legal or illegal, which loses half their revenue, faces a great chance of complete collapse. Our government is running up deficits, spending billions yearly fighting marijuana, and losing billions by not taxing marijuana. There are some who think that the Government should have final say regarding your health; others think the Government should increase more spending to fight marijuana. We need to have this issue in the debates, and have the candidate's state their stance regarding the current disastrous marijuana policy. Sadly many candidates chase the special interest monies, and lobbyists don't always lobby for what is best for the country. Most people think marijuana as drug business, but actually it has far greater economic potentials. The hemp plant (marijuana) has many viable commercial and industrial uses (energy and materials). Did you know that our founding fathers George Washington and Thomas Jefferson grew hemp, and that the Declaration of Independence is written on hemp paper? And for the record, the last three Presidents of the United States of America have smoked marijuana at one time. Finally, how do I really know why marijuana should be legal? The Bible tells me so (Genesis 1:11-13, Genesis 1:29-31). Outlawing a plant that God created is truly Satan's trickery to turn people against God (Psalm 119:81-88, Isaiah 42:5-9). Everything that God created has a purpose (Ezekiel 47:12, Revelation 22:1-5). God gave us the right of free will; even our founding fathers realized this when writing our Constitution. But our government has been slowly eroding these God given rights (Luke 7:28-35, 2 Corinthians 11:1-33). Will our government outlaw the burning of incense in church because of public health concerns? It's now the time to end the prohibition of marijuana. Legalize it, regulate it, and Tax it.

CHAPTER SEVENTEEN:

Get Americans Off The Couch

America needs to get tough on the unemployment problem in the United States. There should be penalties for people that are drawing unemployment that are not willing to work. It is past the time where the government should be backing welfare to those that choose not to take menial jobs that do not pay wages in the amount that they would like. If any unemployed person drawing checks from the government turns down a job that will improve the quality of life in their city they will be immediately dropped from unemployment.

There are many different types of jobs that could be utilized in the support of unemployment. There are many places that have parks that could be taken care of. There is plenty of graffiti that could be removed throughout many cities and litter that could be picked up off of our streets.

I am not advocating the elimination of the unemployment. I believe that there are too many that are abusing the system and not taking jobs that are available. The community service work will clean up America and at the same time make people do something to earn their welfare payments. The American people might be surprised at how many go off the unemployment rolls when they have to do some actual work to receive their unemployment checks. The community service would be on a basis of 30 hours per week so that the individuals would still have time to look for work.

The making people work formula will encourage workers to take jobs that they have been snubbing in favor of extended handouts from the government.

The government needs to send a clear message that if you can work you will be required to work for free while you are drawing your unemployment benefits. There are close to 12 million Americans that are drawing unemployment benefits. Just think how beautiful America will be when we put all those people to work cleaning up our country? The end result will be a reduction in the number of people drawing unemployment due to the fact that they will not want to do the menial jobs that the communities provide. When these unemployment roles decrease we will be making a huge step in reducing the annual budget deficit. The message will be clear. If you can work, then a life of benefits will no longer be an option.

Under these work programs anyone that turns down these community job offers or fails to show up for work will automatically be removed from the unemployment rolls. These changes will not only decrease the annual budget deficit but will get a few million people off the systems that are able to work. Those that are not able to work would not be affected.

The problem of staying on the unemployment system instead of taking low paying jobs will be eliminated. Because our unemployment benefits are often higher than some of the jobs available just encourages people to refuse to take the low paying jobs. What most of the unemployed fail to realize is that a large number of these low paying jobs will lead to much better jobs in the future?

Americans are faced with the problem of accepting the low paying jobs as the benefits are often more than some ordinary jobs pay. Many people hesitate before accepting job offers, or wait until they are no longer eligible for payments.

Watch the civil liberties unions jump on this idea. They are going to say that it is punishment without due process. The fact is that the local and state governments can use the list of recipients drawing unemployment and make them a written offer to perform the community functions. If the unemployed refuses then they will automatically be dropped from the unemployment rolls.

The following comments are from American citizens that have responded to the situation. They are exactly as they were written and are not necessarily my opinion. It will give you an idea about how many Americans feel about the welfare and unemployment programs in the United States.

Wow, you mean the United States could decide that people actually have to try and find jobs after being eligible for benefits? In the city near where I live, you actually see someone pay for something with food stamps, then go outside and climb into a Mercedes. At least our country could get it right. Of course people who need help should get it but so many people have abused the system they give a bad name to the people who actually deserve help and would love to find a job and be a productive citizen.

Too many people when given the choice between a relatively small or modest weekly check with no requirements attached (i.e., work) will choose that over actually getting up at the same time every day and going to the appointed location (i.e., their job). The incentive to not work has to be removed for these people or they will remain content but poor but of their own choosing. Welfare should be what it was designed to be, which is a safety net and not a way of life. There is nothing altruistic in paying people not to work who are otherwise able.

I disagree with the total elimination of welfare, unemployment and Social Security. But total and real reform absolutely!

The United States has been losing its dynamic nature. We were always a country of self sufficient people. You worked and educated yourself to a better life. Almost every ethnic group coming in has worked their way up without handouts the Irish, the Italians, Chinese and Koreans to name a few. Times have changed somewhat but that doesn't preclude people from putting in the effort. People have to take the responsibility for their lives and their choices.

The free ride has to stop. Unemployment is high? During the Depression, thousands were put to work rather than living on the dole. Disability & welfare cheats should be prosecuted.

Let's bring back common sense, mixed in with some compassion, to all these programs. Otherwise we'll go broke.

Simple solution, swap out the illegal immigrants on farms with the ones that have been on welfare for more than two years. I am willing to give the ones new to welfare an opportunity to actually be productive, but anyone on welfare for more than two years can go pick the corn, strawberries, etc. This way they are earning their entitlements, no milking the system. As for the illegals they will be forced to apply for citizenship or go home because there will be no jobs for them.

Wasn't it Nancy Pelosi who said "Extending unemployment benefits is the best way to stimulate the economy" why can we not learn from other country's mistakes? Yes other countries have socialized medicine; they have also lived under the military umbrella proved by us. While we spent on the military, they provided social services. Now that the money is drying up their people are rioting in the streets. Our debt commission is talking about a retirement age of 69, in France they just raised the age to 62 and their people rioted. America is a great nation, but each of us need to make our own way. The Government owes us security, not a monthly paycheck. Work over welfare? I agree with that. I'd bet it would be a big surprise of how many people would find work when they find out they have to work for their welfare and unemployment money.

Too long has the welfare, unemployment and Social Security systems here in the United States been abused. My company has random drug testing rules. I pay taxes that support welfare and unemployment and social security. How about if they take random drug tests....if you fail, you're "fired". Last year, New York State was having trouble coming up with money to keep state parks open...couldn't pay the workers. And yet we paid people to sit home. What would happen if they found out they had to show up to a park and work 3 days a week? The disability system is totally abused....and I blame lawyers with stupid lawsuits.

California proposed work-for-welfare several years ago and it was shot down by self-serving liberals who felt that it wasn't fair to the unemployed. But it's more than fair to make the employed keep paying habitual lazy people to sit around on their fat fannies all day.

The majority of the lower income/welfare recipients are Democratic voters. Pelosi has expanded entitlement programs the past two years. If you took any family of 3 on welfare, and just use the national averages for a year - $14,400.00 just in welfare checks, $6,000.00 Food Stamps, $600.00 Transportation Tokens, and on top get free or reduced rent, and don't pay their utilities. Ever wonder why it cost $16.00 on your electric bill just to get power to your house? The answer is that you are paying for service for some one else. The system is a joke here.

SSI payments are outrageous. These people never paid into the system and there are many, especially adults, who are on it and don't work. They claim that their depression, OCD, Bi-Polar or other crap like that keeps them from working.

I say that is a bunch of garbage. No one in our government: Republican or Democrat will do anything about that. Entitlements are way out of control here and you can see it with people that are perfectly able to walk yet still have a handicap sticker because they complained enough or paid off a doctor to give them one.

Unless you are in a wheel chair, blind (unable to drive because of it), crutches, or walker, you should not be able to collect any benefits as a handicap. Being a fat slob is not enough to claim yourself as a handicap. We need to put a stop to this abuse of the system.

America needs a total welfare reform. Every person who applies for welfare first needs to provide proof of citizenship with ID/birth certificate this alone will cut down on the numbers. We also need monthly drug testing to make sure those on welfare are not on drugs and eligible for a job since most jobs now drug test. Then for those on welfare let's say longer then 6 months are then required to do community service every week at least half of the working hours. Also put a max on the number of eligible kids in the household. Maximum of 2 kids for benefits, this will help ensure those people on welfare with 6 kids and no jobs don't continue to abuse the system while they drive there SUVs to the local Wal-Mart. As a parent I understand kids are a job but as a taxpayer I shouldn't have to pay you for sitting on your hump while you continue to pump out kids you can't afford.

I think it is only common sense that every country should have a system similar to this. You should have to work for your welfare. Anyone that is capable of working but chooses not to then you're not deserving of a handout. You should have to earn what the government gives you, or get nothing at all.

Do you realize how much nicer our cities and towns would be if to get their welfare checks, even if there were no real jobs available, people had to clean graffiti or pick up trash? It would be somewhat like having a job, and would give them incentive to work, or get out.

Yes, I personally know of two families, single women with 6 kids each, that have never had a job. Both are in their late 30's now and have never worked a day in their lives. Both collect welfare, telling the State Human Services that they don't know who the daddies are to all those kids. What a crock, the daddy or daddies are there most of the time! In my state they get $300 cash assistance per child, plus EBT card for groceries, plus subsidized rent and utilities! What a crock, we are paying these women to be baby machines and live better than normal people that work.

Drug testing United States welfare recipients should be a priority. This wasting of tax payer money is foolish. Yet representatives of these people will call the working people the mean spirited who only care for their selves. Wake up people stop this crap.

America needs to do something to correct these abuses on all of the entitlement programs. That money would be better spent on schools, national security, and infrastructure. I don't get extra money from my employer for having more kids; people on welfare shouldn't either if they've been on for more than a few years. They should have to budget for more children, just like the rest of us. That would reduce welfare payments by billions too and we'd have fewer children winding up in the foster care system. Correct these programs and save money all around.

Take the unemployed in California, especially in the Central Valley and put them on graffiti clean up. The parents of the gangsters would be cleaning up their own mess. Also take the chain immigration people on SSI and make them do freeway cleanup. Otherwise, strip them of their benefits.

That should give you an idea about what the American people are actually thinking about the entitlement programs. I am not trying to eliminate programs that are for the people that actually need them. It would be nice to make some changes to these programs that will eliminate all the fraud that is happening within the programs.

CHAPTER EIGHTEEN:

Complete the Border Fence

Stalled Virtual Border Fence

The Department of Homeland Security Janet Napolitano has already frozen work on the controversial virtual fence that was supposed to secure roughly 1,900 miles along the United States border between the United States and Mexico. Reports are out that the Department of Homeland Security is going to cancel the entire program sometime in November 2010.

That is probably the only intelligent thing that Janet Napolitano has proposed during her entire time in that office. Now the Department of Homeland Security needs to understand that the Mexicans have invaded the United States and station our military on the southern border.

The questions that most of the American citizens are asking is why in the world the Department of Homeland Security would hire Boeing to be responsible for securing our borders in the first place. Boeing has enough trouble getting their aircraft produced on schedule. Just how lame brained was this selection anyway? Put the United States Army Corps of Engineers on the job and build a real fence.

The Department of Homeland Security is proposing to increase the number of drones flying along the border. Just look at how effective they have been in Afghanistan after about 10 years of use. Another option would be to increase the number of border patrol agents or rely on the National Guard. The government is hedging on increasing the number of agents due to the 1900 miles of unprotected border. The Department of Homeland Security states that manpower solutions are not cost effective. That is after they have wasted over $1 billion on the program that they intend to scrap. Can anyone figure out these cost effective actions are benefiting our country? Complete the construction of the fence and the America's Highway along the fence which are one time costs. Then the border can be patrolled more efficiently and effectively.

Then if you can believe just how stupid the Department of Homeland Security is they are considering a different type of program that is similar to the one just scrapped. Again with a civilian contractor that is not in the construction business. Starting over with new bids gives the illegals another 24 months of free entry into the United States. How many of the 2 million or more illegals will be terrorists?

The virtual fence should be written off as a very stupid move and move forward with what will be completed in the shortest period of time. The United States is incurring costs because of the illegals at approximately $50 billion per year. How can anyone in government think the cost of the fence is too expensive? Look at the alternative. It is like comparing the problem of getting old compared to dying young.

That brings us to the point. President Bush started the construction of a physical border fence. The Democratic Congress stalled the completion and blamed it on reported legal challenges. It is doubtful that the President would sign any legislation commencing construction of a border fence. The attitude of Janet Napolitano is that is you build a 50 foot fence they will use a 51 foot ladder. What she doesn't understand is that we would have several minutes to use high powered rifles and shoot the illegals while they are climbing the ladder. We would not have to shoot very many and they will take their ladder back to Mexico. That is just another lame excuse by the Department of Homeland Security and Janet Napolitano with the support of President Obama. The Democrats do not want to stop the illegals from entering the United States. There is a hidden agenda to grant amnesty to the 20 plus million illegals that are in the country.

Based on the opinions of President Obama and Janet Napolitano and the rest of the administration we can't stop them so lets just move the border northward about 20 miles per year until they have what they want. Why doesn't someone in the current administration understand that we have military personnel that have the training to defend our borders? We can go all over the world and interfere with other governments and defend their borders. What is the matter with this situation?

People just don't realize how easy it is to cross the border into the United States from Mexico. If you lived in these areas you would realize how sinfully easy it is to make these movements. It is not just an illegal alien issue anymore, national security should be the main goal, so what will it take for people of other countries like Yemen based al-Qaida, terrorist from Iran and others. The United States government is responsible for the nation's borders, instead they're suing the state of Arizona, and other states that are doing what the government is suppose to be doing. It doesn't matter where you live in the United States you should be angry that they're spending taxpayer dollars to go after states that are fighting a border war they should be doing. The only way the citizens are ever going to solve the problem is to send emails and letters every day to the representatives of your local district. Let them know the will of the people and that we will not stand for anything else.

An article from Monterrey, Mexico and reported by Reuters indicated that the Mexican Marines had killed one of the drug lords that was terrorizing the area. The report indicated that this was a victory for President Calderon. The Mexican report indicated that 3 marines and 4 gunmen were killed. It also claimed that a civilian reporter was killed.

This article fails to mention some import information. According to the Valley Morning Star, which is in Harlingen, Texas, not far from Matamoras, stated that there were 47 people killed in this little gun battle? It is suspicious to me that this Reuters report makes is sound like only 8 were killed. Forty seven people being killed in Matamoras is about the same as 47 being killed in Washington, D.C., a city about the same population. Don't you think if 47 were killed in Washington, D.C. that it wouldn't be plastered all over the news? Come on folks, we have a war raging right next door to us and a mainstream news media is failing to report the real news because of their love for President Obama and his administration who finds it more convenient to look the other way.

Every American needs to question ourselves about why President Obama, Senator Reid and the other Democrats refuse to send troops to the borders? Could it be that Reid won Nevada because of the votes in Las Vegas and Reno was funded by money from the drug cartels and unions through the casino industry to support and attract the Hispanic votes?

The border situation has been an ongoing problem for years. The President in recent history that cracked down on illegal immigration was President Eisenhower. Everyone else has ignored it or has been too enamored with Hispanic votes or cheap labor to close the border. Calderon would have you believe that most of the drug cartels weapons came form United States. Try buying a full automatic weapon, grenade, or grenade launcher, and it is evident that these are military grade weapons from other places. Our federal government has proven to be totally useless and will continue to dance around the issue until a real massacre or ambush occurs in the United States. Then they will want to disarm the law-abiding citizens so we are defenseless. Note how robust the European economies are, and how successful they are in dealing with the illegal Muslim immigrants there. Nothing will change until Americans quit doping themselves for fun and recreation, and we quit voting the same party hacks in that kowtow to the same cheap vote and union labor interests. The best part is that the United States is still one of the best places on earth to live. I wonder how long this will last if we continue to allow millions of illegals to enter our wonderful country every year?

The immigration problem of the United States.

How it affects every American.

If I could have "My American Dream" with regards to the immigration problem that the United States of America is struggling with it would go something like the following:

"Close every border and access point into the United States of America. Should the Mexican, Canadian, Cuban or any other government be offended by our border policy that is fine? We can live with that much better than we can live with the illegal migrants into the United States."

"Locate every illegal person that is in the United States of America and take them back to the closet border where they came from. The simple fact is that they are criminals and illegal and are not deserving of any type of protection by our laws."

"This is to include all the anchor babies born in the United States of America during the time that the illegal parents are living in our country."

"Current polls show that approximately 75% to 80% of the legal voting American Citizens are in favor of securing our borders. About the same percentages are in favor of adopting laws similar to the Arizona SB1070."

Is it just me, or does anyone else find it amazing that during the mad cow epidemic our government could track a single cow, born in Canada, almost three years ago, right to the stall where she slept in the State of Washington and they tracked her calves to their stalls? But they are unable to locate 20 million illegals when they wander around our country. Maybe we should give each of them a cow so that we can locate them?

Every American should be proud to salute our flag and be proud to be an American. Thank God for our military that will stand and fight for our freedom and the freedom of the rest of the world. If any one living in this wonderful country does not want to adjust to our way of life then they should go back where they came from.

Proud to be an American and I salute this flag.

CHAPTER NINETEEN:

Wake Up America

The Federal government under the leadership of President Obama and his loyal followers is going to bend over America and really give it to them this time.

The report by the Associated Press is really misleading when it states that the President has a bipartisan deficit commission. There is not a Republican in his right mind that will ever allow this proposal to become law.

Erskine Bowles and former Wyoming Sen. Alan Simpson, co-chairmen of President Barack Obama's bipartisan deficit commission proposed curbs in Social Security benefits, deep reductions in federal spending and higher taxes for millions of Americans to stem a flood of red ink that they said threatens the nation's very future.

The Republican lawmakers had better respond quickly and strongly to the commissions proposals. They include increasing the retirement age for full social security benefits from the current levels to 66 to 69 by the year 2075. The plan would also raise the regular Social Security retirement age to 68 by about 2050 and to 69 in 2075. The full retirement age for those retiring now is 66. For those born in 1960 or after, the full retirement age is now 67.

Besides social security Medicare spending would be curtailed. The tax breaks on many healthcare plans would be eliminated and the deduction for interest on the primary residence of the taxpayer would be eliminated. The commission estimated that these changes would eliminate $4 trillion from the national deficit in the next decade.

This commission is proposing to make changes to programs that have been paid for by the taxpayers for most of their lives and are calling these programs entitlement programs. Mr. Obama these are not entitlement programs they are what the majority of Americans have paid into for 50 years or so and they are retirement programs. Your entitlement programs are the illegals that are bankrupting all levels of government. Those and the 99 weeks of unemployment would eliminate $20 trillion from the federal deficit during the next decade. Where are your priorities? I know, you are looking out for the Hispanic and uneducated to make sure that you will get enough votes for the Democratic Party. How about getting in the Oval office and actually doing some work?

Where in the world does the President find these brain dead loony's that are trying to make policy that will harm just about every citizen of the United States?

In addition to the social security plan increasing the age to full retirements the commission would adopt a program where the current recipients would receive smaller than anticipated annual increases. Just how are they going to lower the increases? The senior citizens of the United States have not received any increases for 2010 and 2011.

Then we have the commission wanting to eliminate the income tax deduction on the mortgages that the taxpayer pays. Why doesn't the government think that this should be considered increasing the income taxes of the majority of taxpayers? This is after the fiasco caused by Fannie Mae and Freddie Mac concerning the mortgage crisis? How many times are the Democrats going to present programs that are going to bury the taxpayers?

The commission acknowledged that these proposals were controversial and would be difficult to pass. No kidding? You want to have 58 million seniors and millions of homeowners bend over to pay for the Democrats spending sprees. Does anyone really think Obama and his committees have any inkling of what they are doing?

The commission stated that the debt is like a cancer on the United States that will truly destroy this country from within if we do not fix it. That is the only good thing that has come from the commission's recommendations. The way to fix the deficit is to cut the spending. President Obama' spending has increased the budget more in the two years he has been in office than all the cuts that are designed to hurt the elderly and working class of Americans.

The government reported separately Wednesday that the deficit for last month alone was $140.4 billion -- and that was 20 percent lower than a year earlier. Wait a minute. If the deficit was $140.4 billion for a month that would indicate that the deficit for the year would be $1,684.8 trillion. The red ink for all of the past fiscal year was $1.29 trillion, second highest on record, and this year is headed for the third straight total above $1 trillion. Current deficits require the government to borrow 37 cents out of every dollar it spends.

When the President decides to quit slamming programs down the taxpayers throats like the healthcare, stimulus, cap and trade to mention a few we will be able to come close to a balanced budget. The Federal government needs to pass legislation that the budget will be balanced every year and what is in excess of the budget will be applied to the deficit.

Some comments from other taxpayers.

How about cutting some people from the Presidents $150k plus government workers hired since he took office? He already has cut benefits for social security and Veterans Affairs benefits for 2 yrs in a row. Government workers that are currently making $150K per year are given a $10k raise. This seems like it could be part of Reverend Wright's agenda against America. We need to vote the pension benefits out of the presidents and congressional payroll and make serving the people what it was meant to be, a service not a retirement.

This is such a crock. After working for 50 years, now they want to cut my benefits. The government is a bunch of thieving irresponsible politicians.

I am sick to death of them all. There must be other programs that can be cut, however about welfare, and kick all those damned illegals out and quit giving them welfare and healthcare. Anyone who votes to cut social security for our retired citizens is going to get their asses handed to them next election. Oh, and by the way, Social Security is not welfare or a government entitlement program, workers have paid into the system for all their working life, and there was no option to opt out, now they want to cut benefits, no way.

Easy, eliminate the cap on social security taxes (currently $104,000) everybody below this pays tax on 100% of our income. Make it fair, eliminate the cap, and social security would be solvent for the next 75-80 years. Unfortunately that means members of Congress would also pay on 100% of the money we pay them. Probably not a go. Also repeal the 2005 law prohibiting the government from bargaining with drug companies for lower prices. According to then-vice president Cheney, this alone tripled the cost of Medicare. Drug companies are making lots though.

We have basically given our wealth to foreign countries.

Bring American jobs home from overseas. Tax overseas profits earned by American companies. Tax imports from foreign countries like they do to our products. Rebuild the manufacturing industry in the United States. Force corporations and unions to work together to rebuild our country. Provide tax credits to Americans buying American products.

I'm really tired of hearing the phrase "entitlement" programs when folks refer to Social Security.... we've paid these taxes for all our working years; they are not merely entitled to us, but owed to us. The lack of a raise for 2010 and 2011 is cruel and unusual punishment when based on "low inflation!" For example, butter is $2.98 a pound, milk over $3.50, and "on-sale" bread over $2.00 -- how are seniors supposed to live on what we get from Social Security, to say nothing about medical needs, shelter, etc. Cutting back and not giving cost of living raises smacks of "age discrimination" which is against the Federal Law. Again, I reiterate, seniors have paid these taxes and they were to have been maintained in a trust. I'm thinking the trust in the federal government is down the tube, based on these decisions.

This is the only country in the world that rewards law breakers. Stop giving free health care, jobs, driver's licenses, education, food stamps and social security benefits to illegal aliens.

At the top of the list should be complete review and reform of the gold-plated compensation and benefit plans of Congress. Second on the list should be complete review and reform of compensation and benefit plans of all other federal employees. The objective in reforming these two areas would be to bring them into line with private sector practices. Then we could start talking about things like reducing federal employment followed by program expenditures, especially military and foreign aid expenditures.

Why don't they reduce the budget by doing away with retirement for federal employees? All the rest of the people working in the United States don't have entitlement retirement systems. How about a 401 the government will give 3% and the employee can give 3%. That would be a good start. Next reduce the government work force and the salary range. A Federal Government employee makes on average $70,000 per year and the average Joe on working in the private sector only makes $40,000. Then there are the people who do nothing but get their dole from the government. Low cost housing, welfare, food stamps, etc. I know of a woman in Georgia who has 14 children and a husband no one can find. She receives $27,000 per year in food stamps that doesn't include federal free food, free housing, and a welfare payment for each child. Where is the Husband? It is time for Change. If the federal government takes away mortgage interest that would be a major tax increase for all home owning Americans and many will lose their homes or more will go into mortgage failure. Wake Up, I think the real Americans want Change less government and fewer taxes.

Of course, first lower social security then raise Medicare premiums, no social security cost of living allowance, raise the social security age to 70. That should put the old people on Welfare. Next, let's hit the young and old home owners that have an interest mortgage and take that away as a deduction. I've not seen one thing about taking something away from our government workers and legislators, or even stopping the money drain for the two wars that are bankrupting this country for the last 12 years. Is this a great run country or what?

And when is the government going to cut its expenses: lower their salaries, reduce inefficient headcount and eliminate pork and earmark spending, sell unneeded real estate, put themselves on Social Security like the rest of us and eliminate their pensions. These should save far more than the $4 trillion.

Simply stop giving our hard earned tax dollars away over seas to any country with a hand out. We just promised millions to Indonesia where the volcano went off. Take care of America and Americans first and the rest second and third down the line. I am tired of supporting the rest of the world let them support themselves. I am tired of fastening my belt up notches for them. Oh, and by the way Congress should take pay cuts and start living like the rest of America. How about stopping the President from spending millions on travel trips. Just how many has he taken to support the Democrats?

That will give everyone an idea of what America thinks of the commission's proposals. These were from 5 minutes of activity by the responding citizens.

Wake Up America – Part II

The same day the President's commission on dealing with the deficit that recommended reducing the salaries of government employees by 10% the President proposed the following pay raise for government employees.

Fox News reported that President Obama has recommended an across the board pay raise of 1.4% for all of the governments 2.1 million employees. In addition, the report stated that the number of employees earning $150K or higher per year has doubled since President Obama took office less than two years ago.

Sure looks like the President is really trying to decrease the deficit by spending and more spending while punishing the American taxpaying citizens. This is really going to make the 58 million senior citizens that are living on social security happy.

Then let's try and compute an example of how the commissions proposal to take away the tax deduction for mortgage interest. To make the example simple we will use a tax deduction of $10,000 in mortgage interest. This taxpayer would have had a $20,000 taxable income after the mortgage deduction. His income tax would have amounted to $2,169.00 if married and filing a joint tax return. If you eliminate the $10,000 deduction his taxable income would jump to $30,000 and the income tax would amount to $3,669.00. The commission was recommending a 3% tax rate deduction. That would save this taxpayer a total of $900.00 on the $30,000 taxable income. Now this is so simple even a caveman can understand. The problem is that the President and his commission can not understand. Take the $3,669.00 and subtract the $900.00 difference in the tax rate and this taxpayer would owe $2,769.00. That indicates that the government has spun the facts. This taxpayer actually had an increase in income taxes in the amount of $600.00 or 3% on his taxable income of $20,000.

Besides hurting every senior citizen these types of policies are hurting every homeowner that has a mortgage. At the same time the President is recommending a pay raise for all government employees.

CHAPTER TWENTY:

Unemployment Expiring

Two million people will run out of unemployment benefits next month if Congress fails to act in the coming weeks. The deadline to file for federal unemployment benefits expires on November 30, 2010. If it is not pushed back, 800,000 people will stop getting checks within four days, according to the National Employment Law Project, an advocacy group.

Unemployment benefits have become a political football, though the national unemployment rate has hovered just below 10% all year. Both parties have previously said they want to lengthen the federal safety net, but Republicans have temporarily blocked extensions several times this year because they do not want to add to the deficit.

It could be even more difficult to push back the deadline this time around now that the Republicans have won control of the House and gained seats in the Senate. Though the transfer of power doesn't happen until next year, Democrats will have to work with the Republicans to craft a bill. The last time the unemployment benefits were extended it added $34 billion to the annual deficit.

House Democrats are expected to push for an extension this month. Republican leaders did not return requests for comment. For the record: Republicans have never been hesitant about supporting unemployment benefits to those who have lost their jobs through no fault of their own. What they have been saying is they want to first identify the means by which continued unemployment benefits can be paid for without raising the deficit.

People forget or fail to realize that most of the unemployed have worked all of their lives and are now in the position of barely keeping what they worked for or have lost it all already. It is not that the majority of the unemployed do not want to work it is that they need to be paid a living wage in order to be able to do so. We've been trying to hire for 2 positions and everyone we've interviewed - when we've called to offer them the job - has said "I don't want to lose my unemployment benefits so sorry, I can't accept the position." What will stop this attitude that it's ok to collect but not ok to work?

There is a lot of work that needs to be done in our country, after the great depression of 29; there were several public programs for folk to earn money. The CCC, civilian conservation corps, built fences and cleaned up waterways and a lot of other things. The Workman's Project Administration put folk to work building sidewalks and roadways and other projects. People got paid to work not to sit around and collect unemployment. Changes need to be made. If people can collect $290.00 per week why work at a job that is going to report the income? These people take scab jobs that are paid in cash just like the illegals.

YOU REAP WHAT YOU SOW:

This short story is for all of those that are unemployed and starting to give up hope. I hope the ones that read it realize there are better days ahead for everyone.

Good morning said a woman as she walked up to the man sitting on ground.

The man slowly looked up.

This was a woman clearly accustomed to the finer things of life. Her coat was new. She looked like she had never missed a meal in her life.

His first thought was that she wanted to make fun of him, like so many others had done before.. "Leave me alone," he growled. To his amazement, the woman continued standing.

She was smiling -- her even white teeth displayed in dazzling rows. "Are you hungry?" she asked.

"No," he answered sarcastically. "I've just come from dining with the president. Now go away."

The woman's smile became even broader. Suddenly the man felt a gentle hand under his arm.

"What are you doing, lady?" the man asked angrily. "I said to leave me alone.

Just then a policeman came up. "Is there any problem, ma'am?" he asked?

"No problem here, officer," the woman answered. "I'm just trying to get this man to his feet. Will you help me?"

The officer scratched his head. "That's old Jack. He's been a fixture around here for a couple of years. What do you want with him?"

"See that cafeteria over there?" she asked. "I'm going to get him something to eat and get him out of the cold for awhile."

"Are you crazy, lady?" the homeless man resisted. "I don't want to go in there!" Then he felt strong hands grab his other arm and lift him up. "Let me go, officer. I didn't do anything."

"This is a good deal for you, Jack" the officer answered. "Don't blow it."

Finally, and with some difficulty, the woman and the police officer got Jack into the cafeteria and sat him at a table in a remote corner. It was the middle of the morning, so most of the breakfast crowd had already left and the lunch bunch had not yet arrived.

The manager strode across the cafeteria and stood by his table. "What's going on here, officer?" he asked. "What is all this, is this man in trouble?"

"This lady brought this man in here to be fed," the policeman answered.

"Not in here!" the manager replied angrily. "Having a person like that here is bad for business."

Old Jack smiled a toothless grin. "See, lady. I told you so. Now if you'll let me go. I didn't want to come here in the first place."

The woman turned to the cafeteria manager and smiled. "Sir, are you familiar with Eddy and Associates, the banking firm down the street?"

"Of course I am," the manager answered impatiently. "They hold their weekly meetings in one of my banquet rooms."

"And do you make a goodly amount of money providing food at these weekly meetings?"

"What business is that of yours?"

I, sir, am Penelope Eddy, president and CEO of the company."

"Oh."

The woman smiled again. "I thought that might make a difference." She glanced at the cop who was busy stifling a giggle. "Would you like to join us in a cup of coffee and a meal, officer?"

"No thanks, ma'am," the officer replied. "I'm on duty."

"Then perhaps, a cup of coffee to go?"

"Yes, that would be very nice."

The cafeteria manager turned on his heel, "I'll get your coffee for you right away, officer."

The officer watched him walk away. "You certainly put him in his place," he said.

"That was not my intent. Believe it or not, I have a reason for all this."

She sat down at the table across from her amazed dinner guest. She stared at him intently. "Jack, do you remember me?"

Old Jack searched her face with his old, rheumy eyes. "I think so -- I mean you do look familiar."

"I'm a little older perhaps," she said. "Maybe I've even filled out more than in my younger days when you worked here, and I came through that very door, cold and hungry."

"Ma'am?" the officer said questioningly. He couldn't believe that such a magnificently turned out woman could ever have been hungry.

"I was just out of college," the woman began. "I had come to the city looking for a job, but I couldn't find anything. Finally I was down to my last few cents and had been kicked out of my apartment. I walked the streets for days. It was February and I was cold and nearly starving. I saw this place and walked in on the off chance that I could get something to eat."

Jack lit up with a smile. "Now I remember," he said. "I was behind the serving counter. You came up and asked me if you could work for something to eat. I said that it was against company policy."

"I know," the woman continued. "Then you made me the biggest roast beef sandwich that I had ever seen, gave me a cup of coffee, and told me to go over to a corner table and enjoy it.. I was afraid that you would get into trouble... Then, when I looked over and saw you put the price of my food in the cash register, I knew then that everything would be all right."

"So you started your own business?" Old Jack said.

"I got a job that very afternoon. I worked my way up. Eventually I started my own business that, with the help of God, prospered." She opened her purse and pulled out a business card.. "When you are finished here, I want you to pay a visit to a Mr. Lyons. He's the personnel director of my company. I'll go talk to him now and I'm certain he'll find something for you to do around the office." She smiled. "I think he might even find the funds to give you a little advance so that you can buy some clothes and get a place to live until you get on your feet... If you ever need anything, my door is always opened to you."

There were tears in the old man's eyes. "How can I ever thank you?" he said.

"Don't thank me," the woman answered. "To God goes the glory. Thank Jesus... He led me to you."

Outside the cafeteria, the officer and the woman paused at the entrance before going their separate ways.

"Thank you for all your help, officer," she said.

"On the contrary, Ms. Eddy," he answered. "Thank you. I saw a miracle today, something that I will never forget. And thank you for the coffee."

If you have missed knowing me, you have missed nothing.

If you have missed some of my emails, you might have missed a laugh.

But, if you have missed knowing my Lord and Savior, Jesus Christ, you have missed everything in the world.

Have a Wonderful Day. May God Bless you always and don't forget that when you "cast your bread upon the waters," you never know how it will be returned to you.

God is so big He can cover the whole world with his Love and so small He can curl up inside your heart.

When God leads you to the edge of the cliff, trust Him fully and let go.

Only 1 of 2 things will happen, either He'll catch you when you fall, or He'll teach you how to fly!

The power of one sentence!

God is going to shift things around for you today and let things work in your favor.

God closes doors no man can open & God opens doors no man can close.

If you need God to open some doors for you...have everyone you know read this.

Have a blessed day and remember to be a blessing.

LIVE WELL, LOVE MUCH, LAUGH OFTEN

CHAPTER TWENTY ONE:

Respect for Obama

Respect for the office of President of the Unites States? Yes.

Respect the Man in the Office? No, I am sorry to say.

I have noted that many elected officials, both Democrats and Republicans, called upon America to unite behind Obama.

Well, I want to make it clear to all who will listen that I am not uniting behind President Obama.

I will respect the Office which he holds, and I will acknowledge his abilities as an orator and wordsmith and pray for him, but that is it. I have begun today to see what I can do to make sure that he is a one-term President.

I am doing this because I do not share the majority of his beliefs. I do not agree with Obama on his abortion beliefs. I do not share Obama's vision or value system for America. I do not share his radial Marxist's concept of distributing from the wealthy and giving to the poor. I believe every individual should earn his keep and contribute to the society they live in. I do not share his beliefs that we should raise the taxes on some Americans just because they were successful. I do not think that America is arrogant. I believe that America is a Christian nation under God. I do not want to reduce the size of our military. They have protected our great nation for overt 200 years. Instead we should salute any member of the military every time we meet one. I certainly do not agree that amnesty should be given to any illegal. Each and every illegal in the United States needs to be deported and not given any type of amnesty.

I do not believe that radical Islam is our friend and that Israel is our enemy who should give up any land under any circumstances. I did not like the way Obama crammed the healthcare program down the throats of the citizens without any concern for what they wanted. I definitely do not share the President's plan to sit down with Iran or any other terrorist regime. We have enough terrorists coming across the southern borders of the United States because Obama will not do anything to secure them.

The Democrats have not moved toward the center in their beliefs and their philosophies, and they never came together nor compromised their personal beliefs for the betterment of our Country. They have portrayed my America as a land where everything is tolerated except being intolerant.

I am sure many of you who read this think that I am going overboard, but I refuse to retreat one more inch in favor of those whom I believe are the embodiment of Evil. President Bush made many mistakes during his Presidency, and I am not sure how history will judge him. However, I believe that he weighed his decisions in light of the long established Christian principles of our Founding Fathers.

Majority rules in America. I will honor the concept; however, I will fight with all of my power to be a voice in opposition to Obama and his goals for America. I am going to be a thorn in the side of those who, if left unchecked, will destroy our Country. Any more compromise is more defeat. I pray that the results of this election will wake up many who have sat on the sidelines and allowed the crowd to slowly change so much of what has been good in America. God bless you and God bless our Country.

Why is Obama, the Illinois Democrat, the worst president in history, far surpassing the previous record holder -- Jimmy Carter, the Georgia Democrat? Unfortunately, history does seem to repeat itself. The people elected Jimmy Carter who did not have any experience in government and then repeated the process by electing Barrack Obama who did not have any business or government experience. For the record, being a community organizer does not count as business experience. Don't you think it is about time that the American people try to elect people that have some experience and are qualified?

Obama likes to blame the Republicans for everything. The Democrats had the majority for over two years and they still did nothing. All they were worried about was pushing through Obamacare that the majority of the American people did not want. The reason he is making appointments during a recess is because they would not pass through otherwise.

They are probably more Czars and even the public is sick of them. Something needs to be done before this President destroys America. Has any thought been given to the fact that he snubbed Israel because his true Muslim attitude is starting to show? He bows to Muslims kings but treats the Prime Minister from Israel like scum. Israel has been America's friends for decades. He demands that Israel stop building homes for their people but lets Iran keep building nukes. I believe he has his priorities backwards. In November, the American people voted to replace some of these corrupt politicians. We need to demand that President Obama show his birth certificate and his college records. All other Presidents have had too. Why is he getting shown special treatment? After all, The President is working for the American People, or is he?

The reasons that I believe Mr. Obama is going to be the worst President that has ever held the office in the United States are:

Obama promised to close Gitmo, it is still in operation.

He has treated terrorists as petty criminals. He hasn't tried them in military tribunals for their war crimes. Obama is inexperienced.

Obama policies have tripled the American debt creating obligations that will be taxing children who aren't yet born (remember no taxation without representation? – maybe politicians should not be able to place debt on future generations). Obama is incompetent.

The President from Illinois has supported programs that have lost 2 million jobs, permanently, according to Joe Biden, the Delaware Democratic

Vice President. "It's the economy stupid." President Obama is a clueless concerning unemployment.

Obama promised an open and transparent debate on his policies. A great example is the Obamacare program, but delivered gangster-style, heavy-handed Chicago politics instead. There was not any transparency.

The President has bungled the economy.

Obama talked down America in foreign speeches. Obama is incompetent and reacts to foreign policies before the American peoples desires.

He promised an open and transparent administration. Instead we have back door Chicago politics.

Obama has failed to create jobs. Obama is incapable of supporting business programs to develop more jobs.

The President from Illinois gave a $1 trillion bailout to big business and banks, those who contributed the most to his election.

He has failed to hold unemployment to 8%, as promised: "It's the economy stupid." Obama is incompetent.

The President has bowed to every dictator he met. Obama is inexperienced.

Obama botched the management of the worst environmental disaster in history. Watch, he will take credit for capping the well.

He met in closed session with BP to get $20B. Maybe he could have gotten $100B if the meeting was in the open. Who was paid off?

Obama treats the American people with contempt. Obama does not listen to the will of the people he should have sworn to protect.

Obama has spent more time on vacationing and playing golf wasting his administration away during the oil spill and Christmas bombing attempt in Detroit. Obama is incompetent.

KKK leader Senator Byrd gets a state funeral that Obama attended. Obama honored and eulogized Byrd. Too bad Stalin, Mao Zedong, and Hitler didn't die on his watch Obama would have loved those three.

Obama is an embarrassment to America.

CHAPTER TWENTY TWO:

America's Resources

The following exerts from pages 29 -30 of the Presidents federal budget for 2011.

Eliminate Funding for Inefficient Fossil Fuel Subsidies.

As we work to create a clean energy economy, it is counterproductive to spend taxpayer dollars on incentives that run counter to this national priority. To further this goal, the Budget eliminates tax preferences and funding for programs that provide inefficient fossil fuel subsidies that impede investment in clean energy sources and undermine efforts to deal with the threat of climate change. We are eliminating 12 tax breaks for oil, gas, and coal companies, closing loopholes to raise nearly $39 billion over the next decade.

This kind of rhetoric in the budget is coming at a time where a majority of the American citizens are calling for a balanced budget and the reduction of the wasteful spending of the Obama administration. Clean energy will be wonderful when we reduce the federal deficit which is being caused in large part by the demand for foreign oil in the United States. The President is calling for a cut in the tax breaks for the only people that have the expertise and capital to actually save our country. Why would the President want to take away the only means that American has to reduce our annual deficit?

Boost Development of Clean Energy on Federal and Tribal Land.

Already, public lands and offshore resources managed by the Federal Government constitute about one-third of the domestic supply of fossil fuel resources. The Administration will promote the development of clean, renewable energy on Federal lands. To that end, the Budget adds $14 million—on top of $50 million in 2010 increases—to build agency capacity to review and permit renewable energy projects on Federal lands. This includes conducting the environmental evaluations and technical studies needed to spur development of renewable energy projects, assessing available alternative resources, and mitigating the impacts of development. In addition, the Administration is assisting Indian Tribes in overcoming the unique hurdles in developing renewable resources on Native American lands. Up to 15 percent of our potential wind energy resources are on Native

American land and the potential for solar energy are even higher.

What the American people would like to know is why the President is not pushing to explore for oil and gas reserves on the federal land? It has been proven that the country has enough natural resources in the Rocky Mountain Region and the wilderness of Alaska to supply all the countries needs for the next 30 to 40 years. Tell the environmentalists that they need to start looking out for America instead of trying to protect the Caribou calving grounds or some trees. The way it is going they will not need to worry about protecting these areas because they will be owned by China and they will start exploring for the natural resources right away.

CHAPTER TWENTY THREE

Some of My Newsletters

I have been writing newsletters for quite some time and I am going to enclose some of my favorites into this book. All of my newsletters were available on my website and are free of charge. The web site address is: www.my-american-dream.org

I write these newsletters to point out that it is amazing that the elected members of the Senate and the House of Representatives can not come up with some of the solutions to the United States problems. We are flooded with illegals, our economy is in the worst shape imaginable, unemployment has been in the 9.5% range for too long, healthcare has been implemented, stimulus programs and cap and trade. Most of these programs that have been passed were against the will of the majority of the voting citizens of the United States of America. It is past time for the citizens of the United States to demand that the President, Senate and House of Representatives start enacting programs that the American people want and demand.

MY AMERICAN DREAM

Newsletter
Volume 2010-41

November 12, 2010
www.my-american-dream.org

IN SEARCH OF THE TRUTH:

We as citizens of the United States are demanding the truth from our President. Why would you spend close to $1 million to hide your birth certificate and educational records?

There have been so many e-mails coming these days that I'm beginning to feel we are all getting paranoid about what is going on in government. However, I did look up these documents in the Supreme Court and confirmed that Kagan was Obama's counsel in these cases. I received an e-mail back in January that exposed Scopes as being liberal, but doubt kept me from forwarding on that one. Now I feel confident to do so, so you will receive it also from me.

In our Search for the truth we have that we have suspected on many occasions. People went to Snoops to check this out and they said it was false and there were no such dockets so they 'Googled' the Supreme Court, typed in 'Obama-Kagan,' and guess what? Yep you got it. Snoops lied. Every one of those dockets are there, So Here is what the people wrote to Snoops:

Referencing the article about Elena Kagan and Barak Obama dockets: The information you have posted stating that there were no such cases as claimed and the examples you gave are blatantly false. We went directly to the Supreme Court's website, typed in Obama Kagan and immediately came up with all of the dockets that the article made reference to. We have long suspected that you really slant things but this was really shocking.

Thank You, We hope you will be much more truthful in the future.

****

That being said, we'll bet you didn't know this?

Kagan was representing Obama in all the petitions to prove his citizenship. Now she may help rule on them.

Folks, this is really ugly Chicago Politics; and the beat goes on and on and on. Once again the United States Senate sold us out!

Well, someone figured out why Obama nominated Elena Kagan for the Supreme Court. Pull up the Supreme Courts website and go to the docket and search for Obama.

Kagan was the Solicitor General for all the suits against him filed with the Supreme Court to show proof of natural born citizenship. He owed her big time. All of the requests were denied of course. They were never heard. It just keeps getting deeper and deeper, doesn't it? The American people mean nothing any longer. It's all about payback time for those who compromised themselves to elect someone that really has no true right to even be there. I have copied three examples of the cases that were thrown out by the courts. You can see that the one and only Elena Kagan is the attorney representing Obama.

**If you are not interested in justice or in truth delete this However,
If you hold sacred the freedoms granted to you by the
United States Constitution…
By all means, please… Make sure that
everyone you know reads this.**

The following documents were downloaded from the records of the Supreme Court of the United States of America.

What could be the reason that the President is so set on hiding everything about his birth certificate and educational background? The American people really would like to know.

Supreme Court of the United States

No. 09-6790

Title: Gary William Holt, Petitioner

v.

Barack H. Obama, President of the United States, et al.

Docketed: October 1, 2009

Lower Ct: United States Court of Appeals for the District of Columbia Circuit

Case Nos.: (08-5389)

Decision Date: March 26, 2009

Rehearing Denied: May 15, 2009

~~~Date~~~~~~~~~~~Proceedings and Orders~~~~~~~~~~~~~

Aug 10 2009	Petition for a writ of certiorari and motion for leave To proceed in forma pauperis filed. (Response due November 2, 2009)
Oct 13 2009	Waiver of right of respondents Barack H. Obama, President of the United States, et al. to respond filed.
Oct 22 2009	DISTRIBUTED for Conference of November 6, 2009.
Nov 9 2009	Petition DENIED.

~~Name~~~~~~~~~~~~~~~   ~~Address~~~~~~~~~~~~   ~~Phone~~~~~~

Attorneys for Petitioner:

Gary William Holt
33069-138
Unit- Shelby B
PO Box 34550
Memphis, TN 38184-0550

Party name: Gary William Holt

Attorneys for Respondents:

Elena Kagan
Solicitor General   (202) 514-2217
United States
Department of Justice
950 Pennsylvania
Avenue, N.W.
Washington, DC 20530-0001
SupremeCtBriefs@USDOJ.gov

Party: Barack H. Obama, President of the United States, et al.

Supreme Court of the United States

No. 09-8857

Title:	Jerome Julius Brown, Sr., Petitioner
	v.
	Barack H. Obama, President of the United States, et al.
Docketed:	January 29, 2010
Lower Ct:	United States Court of Appeals for the District of Columbia Circuit
Case Nos.:	(09-5103)
Decision	October 28, 2009

~~~Date~~~~~~~~~~~Proceedings and Orders~~~~~~~~~~~~~

Nov 18 2009	Petition for a writ of certiorari and motion for leave to proceed in forma pauperis filed. (Response due March 1, 2010)
Feb 16 2010	Waiver of right of respondents Barack H. Obama, President of the United States, et al. to respond filed.
Mar 11 2010	DISTRIBUTED for Conference of March 26, 2010.
Mar 29 2010	Petition DENIED.

--Name~~~~~~~~~~~~~~~   --Address~~~~~~~~~~~~~   --Phone~~~~~~

Attorneys for Petitioner:

Jerome Julius Brown Sr.   7209 Robin Hood Drive   (301) 357-9336
                            # 3093
                            Upper Marlboro, MD 20773

Party name: Jerome Julius Brown, Sr.

Attorneys for Respondents:

Elena Kagan   Solicitor General   (202) 514-2217

Counsel of Record   United States Department of Justice
                            950 Pennsylvania Avenue, N.W.
                            Washington, DC 20530-0001
                            SupremeCtBriefs@USDOJ.gov

Party name: Barack H. Obama, President of the United States, et al.

Statue of Liberty

--Name~~~~~~~~~~~~~~~   --Address~~~~~~~~~~~~~   --Phone~~~~~~

Attorneys for Petitioner:

James Bopp Jr.   Bopp, Coleson & Bostrom   (812) 232-2434
                             1 South Sixth Street
                             Terre Haute, IN 47807-3510
                             jboppjr@aol.com

Party name: The Real Truth About Obama, Inc.

Attorneys for Respondents:

Elena Kagan   Solicitor General   (202) 514-2217
                             United States Department of Justice
                             950 Pennsylvania Avenue, N.W.
                             Washington, DC 20530-0001
                             SupremeCtBriefs@USDOJ.gov

Party name: Federal Election Commission, et al.

GOD BLESS AMERICA

MY AMERICAN DREAM

Newsletter   November 2, 2010
Volume 2010-34   www.my-american-dream.org

Happy Election Day! With some luck we will be able to take back the House of Representatives and make headway into the Senate. In today's news there were three more Americans murdered just across the Mexican border.

The federal government does not have any sense what so ever. They are so blind when it concerns something that the vast majority of the American citizens really care about. How many American citizens have to be murdered in Mexico before the President stops suing Arizona and starts enforcing the federal laws regarding illegals? Has the President ever read any part of our immigration laws or the Constitution?

The United States has thousands of military personnel stationed close to the border and yet he is too stupid to use any of them to protect our country. The President would rather bow down to Calderon than stand up for the American citizens. The military has the technology to locate every drug cartel stronghold and eliminate it within 24 hours. What is the reason that the President will not do anything to address our border problems? We need to load the weapons and fire at will on every drug cartel. They are killing the Americans with their constant flow of illegals and drugs. It would be so simple even a caveman could do it.

GOD BLESS AMERICA

MY AMERICAN DREAM

Newsletter   September 16, 2010
Volume 2010-23   www.my-american-dream.org

Well, the Democrats have succeeded in putting it to the American tax payer again. Passing their latest $30 billion will not have any positive effect in lowering the unemployment in the United States. When will they ever learn that spending does not create jobs? The primary focus on this bill is to provide funds to independent community banks to encourage lending to small businesses. When is Obama going to learn from the previous stimulus bills that it does not increase employment or lending to small businesses or individuals.

This bill will work exactly as the previous bill. The independent community banks will not use the funds to loan to small businesses. That is just a ruse to get more of their voters in line because they are looking very bleak with the upcoming election on November 2, 2010. The $12 billion in tax breaks in the bill will not benefit 1% of the small businesses in the United States. Small Businesses do not sell their stock so the tax break is nothing but some more wind being blown by Mr. Obama. The current rules for depreciation and expanding business are more than adequate.

Passing this bill was just another way that the Democrats are trying to fool the American taxpayer and try to salvage to some of the losses that are projected in November. We have known many small businesses and they can tell you that there is nothing in this bill that will help them. When you operate a small business you will not be willing to borrow money because they are already struggling and the last thing any of them will want to do is go further into debt. Businesses will hire more employees when their demand for products or services require. Only a fool would hire unless there was positive indications that these employees would be providing enough profits to justify the costs. Businesses pay payroll taxes, Medicare, insurance and other benefits that are incurred for each employee they hire. It is not just the cost of the salary or wages that affects the businessman. You can figure that it takes about 20% in addition to the salary or wages.

To give everyone a summary of what this $30 billion program will cost divide the number by the 500,000 jobs that it is speculated to provide and you have a very large cost per job created of $60,000? It seems that there are much better ways of creating jobs than spending $60,000 each. That figure might be considerably low because this bill will not stimulate the creation of that many jobs. Once again the President and his lemmings are trying to create the impression that they are doing something to influence more voters to vote Democrat in November. What a crock. When are we as voting taxpayers going to take back our country?

Let's explore what the major cause of why jobs are going to keep being lost in America.

Here's the deal. You're going to start a business or expand the one you've got now. It doesn't really matter what you do or what you're going to do. I'll partner with you no matter what business you're in – as long as it's legal. But we can't give you any capital – you have to come up with that on your own. We won't give you any labor – that's definitely up to you. What we will do, however, is demand you follow all sorts of rules about what products and services you can offer, how much (and how often) you pay your employees, and where and when you're allowed to operate your business. That's my role in the affair: to tell you what to do. Now in return for my rules, we're going to take roughly half of whatever you make in the business each year. Half seems fair, doesn't it? We think so. Of course, that's half of your profits. You're also going to have to pay me about 12% of whatever you decide to pay your employees because you've got to cover my expenses for promulgating all of the rules about who you can employ, when, where, and how. Come on, you're my partner. It's only "fair." Now... after you've put your hard-earned savings at risk to start this business, and after you've worked hard at it for a few decades (paying me my 50% or a bit more along the way each year), you might decide you'd like to cash out – to finally live the good life. Whether or not this is "fair" – some people never can afford to retire – is a different argument. As your partner, We're happy for you to sell whenever you'd like... because our agreement says, if you sell, you have to pay me an additional 20% of whatever the capitalized value of the business is at that time.

We know that you put up all the original capital. You took all the risks. You put in all of the labor. That's all true. But we've done our part, too. We've collected 50% of the profits each year. And we've always come up with more rules for you to follow each year. Therefore, we deserve another, final 20% slice of the business.

All in all, if you're a very successful entrepreneur... if you're one of the rare, lucky, and hard-working people who can create a new company, employ lots of people, and satisfy the public... you'll end up paying us more than 75% of your income over your life. Thank you so much. I'm sure you'll think our offer is reasonable and happily partner with us... but it doesn't really matter how you feel about it because if you ever try to stiff us – or cheat us on any of my fees or rules we will send the Internal Revenue Service after you and harass you the rest of your life. That's how civil society is supposed to work, right? This is America, isn't it? That's the offer America gives its entrepreneurs. And the idiots in Washington wonder why there are no new jobs?

Here is an example of the incredible spending sprees that the Obama and his lemmings have splurged on. House Republicans are collecting photos from the citizens all over the country. These photos are showing that the program has wasted an idiotic sum of $192 million in taxpayer money to plaster every possible highway with signs touting how the stimulus cash is "Putting America to Work" with infrastructure projects. This is a total waste of the taxpayer's money. About the only jobs it created were to Mr. Obama's union buddies. Did it really create any new jobs that were not for the benefit of the unions?

Unfortunately, the vast majority of people in this country have never experienced first hand what it's like to try and start a business, and is completely and totally clueless about the harsh reality. The United States government isn't the solution, it's the problem.

What about the amazing way that Obama and Democrats can continue with these phony policies. The $26 billion bailout money to "save" teachers jobs was not really for that. Almost none of the school districts who got the money "rehired" any teachers. By the time they passed this bill, the districts had already made adjustments and their school year had already started. We are guessing it went to the teacher's pensions and unions. The really sad thing is that the Democrats don't even have a clue what is really in any bill... if Obama says "pass it".... they blindly obey him. Two good examples of this are...Obamacare where Pelosi said "we have to pass it to know what's in it." The Financial "reform" bill - Dodd said "we won't know the impact of this bill until we pass it and apply these regulations."

MY AMERICAN DREAM

Newsletter   October 25, 2010
Volume 2010-31   www.my-american-dream.org

We are going to try and figure out whether the rich are providing their share of the tax burden to the United States of America. We hear so much about how the ultra rich are going to donate 50% of their wealth to charity. What about paying some income or gift or estate tax to the federal government?

For the sake of not offending any of the extremely wealthy we will use Waldo Freeloader as the rich citizen. Waldo Freeloader accumulated the bulk of his $5 billion in wealth from starting a company in America. He received 50 million shares when American Dream, Inc. was founded in 2005. When Waldo founded the Company he had invested a total of $25,000. After creating a great product that was highly successful the American Dream, Inc. decided to take the company public. The offering was a huge success and the Company raised $20 million. The public received 10 million shares at $2.00 per share. Waldo still owned the majority of the company. Waldo still controlled 83.33% of the Company after the public offering was completed.

After several huge successes the price of the Company's shares went to $100 per share. Now Waldo has had the value of his shares increase to $5 billion. Since the price was now to expensive for most investors the Company decides to do a stock split to lower the price to $20.00 per share. This will require a 5 for 1 split. Now Waldo has hit the jackpot.

He now has a total of 250 million shares with a value of his stock in American Dream, Inc. is not worth $5 billion. It is time to be grateful and start giving it to charity.

During the years that American Dream, Inc. was creating this huge amount of wealth Waldo was living the good life from his earnings as the Chief Executive of the Company. Waldo has not had to sell any of his shares.

It would be nice to know just how much gift taxes are going to be paid by Waldo when he gives the wealth to charity. We are going to assume that the gifts to charity are in the form of stock in American Dream, Inc. If Waldo was required to sell the shares and then donate the proceeds it would create income taxes on the sale and the gift. So it is pretty obvious that the gift would be in stock. What Waldo is doing is evading the tax on the gain of his stock and paying the income tax on the gain. Yes, it is very smart on Waldo's part but not in the best interest of the taxpayers.

What we need to do is make sure that Waldo has filed the proper gift tax forms and paid the taxes so that the government receives some of his charity.

Possibly a new piece of legislation should be enacted to change the charitable laws to only allow the gift of cash or property other than stock in publicly traded companies. This would require the sale of the shares before the contribution could be made and therefore the income taxes on the huge gains that taxpayers like Waldo would have to pay. You can hear the screams of the rich already. The charitable organizations will be screaming that they are not receiving their fair share because the donations would be lower.

We also need to consider whether the charitable contribution remains in the United States. We agree that it is great to address world problems but we have way too many serious problems in the United States. Another thing we need to make sure of is that until the law is changed we need to make sure that if a contribution is made with stock that it is valued at the current market price and not what Waldo paid for it. The gift tax rate tops out at 35% for anything over $500,000. If a gift of 1 million shares of American Dream, Inc. stock was made with the current market value of $20.00 the gift would be worth $20 million. If the cost was used as a basis the gift would have been $500.00. The cost to the taxpayers of the United States would be $7 million.

GOD BLESS AMERICA

MY AMERICAN DREAM

Newsletter   October 1, 2010
Volume 2010-31   www.my-american-dream.org

What we can do to manage the unemployment?

If I could have "My American Dream" with regards to the unemployment problem that the United States of America is struggling with it would go something like the following:

"The first major legislation that I would recommend would be to place a payroll tax on every corporation that is exporting jobs to Mexico, Canada, China, Russia, Japan or any other country. This payroll tax would be paid to the Treasury on a monthly basis the same as the normal payroll taxes are paid. The rate of the payroll tax should be 75% of all the wages paid to employees in a foreign country. This would place a very large demand upon the corporations to bring the jobs back into the United States and would be a major factor in improving the unemployment picture as well as the economy."

"The unemployment picture will change very quickly when the United States starts enforcing the laws regarding illegal migrants that are taking 12,000,000 to 15,000,000 jobs. Approximately 2% – 3% of these jobs are in farming and the rest are jobs that most Americans trained and able fill."

"The real unemployment in the United States is more like 20% -25% when you factor in the unemployed that have finished receiving their checks, the part time workers that are unable to locate a full time job, those that were self employed and had their business closed do to lack of business."

"I would like to see the unemployment figures drop to the 5% -6% ranges by implementing the tax on foreign labor and sending the illegal migrants back to their home country."

"We could start employing temporary workers to implement the transfer and deportation of all the illegal migrants and their families."

MY AMERICAN DREAM

Newsletter   October 20, 2010
Volume 2010-21   www.my-american-dream.org

On our website we had posted some of the things that we would recommend to the government to fix the real estate problems in the United States. We have placed them in this newsletter. On September 15, 2010, the Associated Press published an article stating that ("Government say banks should share Fannie, Freddie costs") please excuse them for their lousy English in their headline.

"As much as it would hurt the economy, the United States should let Freddie Mac and Fannie Mae go through a complete liquidation and then force them into bankruptcy. I agree it would create a short term burden on the taxpayers but in the long run it will force the mortgage companies and other lending institutions to make mortgages to qualified individuals"

"Every American would like to own their home. We have to be practical with regards to purchasing a home. Lending institutions need to do due diligence to make sure that the buyer has an adequate down payment, verified income to support the payments, a credit history of making payments on time and purchasing a home that they can afford."

"The lending institutions that made the loans to the unqualified home purchasers should be required to incur the losses from these improper loans. The made the loans knowing that the purchaser would not have the means to pay the mortgage after the ARM kicked in. It was not their concern so they processed a loan that they knew they were going to sell to another mortgage company and then to a Freddie Mac and Fannie Mae guarantee."

"The institution that packaged these mortgages to Freddie Mac and Freddie Mae need to share in these loses. When these institutions incur losses that could put them out of business that is the way it should be. There will always be lending institutions that operate in a manner to make profits without taking undue risk. These institutions really loved the easy profits that were made illegally. It is time to make them realize what they did and make them suffer the consequences."

Did Edward DeMarco, the acting director for the Federal Housing Finance Agency read our website? We have stated all along that the banks have an obligation to pay the cost for bailing out mortgage buyers Fannie Mae and Freddie Mac because they sold them the bad mortgages that the Carter and Clinton administrations requiring the policy to make homes available to every American. That in it self did not tell the banks and mortgage institutions to loan to people regardless of their credit rating and ability to repay the loan.

Instead of caring what will happen to the taxpayer if the banks are not held responsible for the loans that they sold to Fannie Mae and Freddie Mac the government and Wall Street are concerned about what will happen to the banks. Quite frankly, who really cares what happens to the earning of the banks or Wall Street? Reports are that the banks could incur book losses of up to $42 billion if they are forced to repurchase the bad loans they sold to Fannie Mae and Freddie Mac. Wouldn't it be better for the banks that made the bad loans suffer the losses they forced upon Fannie Mae and Freddie Mac? Sources indicate that J. P. Morgan, Chase & Co., Citigroup, Inc., Bank of America and Wells Fargo & Co. could record $17 billion in losses if they repurchase a quarter of the mortgage giant's seriously delinquent loans.

Just think how big these company's losses are going to be when they actually report how many delinquent loans are on their books on real estate that they have not reported. It is not any wonder that the mortgage lending has been so futile. The institutions do not want to show the losses that they would have to take to refinance most of their loans. Could that underscore the fact that only 400,000 loans have been refinanced out of the 10,000,000 foreclosures?

It could all be a conspiracy on the banks part. If they do not loan money to purchase the houses that they have in their foreclosure portfolio then they can drive the prices down further. When they feel like the prices can not go any lower they will start buying these properties back and make the real estate market go higher again. Why is it that history always repeats itself? Isn't what the banks did during the depression of 1929?

One of the things that can be done to stop this is to force every bank to make a full disclosure of the loans in their portfolio. This disclosure will be required to show how many of them are underwater, past due on the payments, in foreclosure, current on the payments and current ration of loan value to the value of the property. The banks must report how many loans that are delinquent and that they have not started foreclosure proceedings on and when they intend to start. The banking industry must be required to make full disclosure on the value of their portfolios. They are currently reporting huge profits but if they were honest about their real estate situation would they be making these profits. If they are they can afford to accept the responsibility for the bad loans that they sold to Fannie Mae and Freddie Mac.

GOD BLESS AMERICA

MY AMERICAN DREAM

Newsletter   September 20 2010
Volume 2010-30   www.my-american-dream.org

According to the main stream media the recession ended in June 2009, making it the longest downturn since World War Two, the National Bureau of Economic Research said on Monday.

The NBER, considered the arbiter of U.S. recessions, said it chose that month based on examination of data including gross domestic product, employment and personal income.

This has to be the worst and most hollow story that we have ever read on Yahoo! News. How do they define 'recession? What is our normal unemployment rate and how do today's numbers compare to that average? How much debt have we accumulated in the last year? What are the housing values and the number in foreclosure? These are all important questions not even mentioned in the article. Show us the metrics.

What is amazing is that Yahoo News would even report such drivel. This appears to be another attempt by the Obama administration to blow smoke up the citizens again to try and gain a few votes. Anyone with an ounce of common sense knows that the recession is not over and more than likely has turned into a very serious depression. The Obama administration has been operating under the false assumption that if you tell a lie often enough that the people will believe it.

The mainstream media has to be kidding. Some of the more obvious statistics reveal that the recession has not ended. Consider the fact that unemployment is being reported by the administration and the mainstream media at 9.6%. The real number when you consider all the facts would be in the range of 16% to 20%.

The value of most homes in America has decreased in some areas by over 50%. There have been about 8 million jobs lost and the economy is not creating enough jobs to even keep up with the population demand which is about 400,000 new jobs per month. The Obama administration has not presented any programs that will provide incentives for companies to increase manufacturing and produce "Made in the USA" products. The value of Americans 401K retirement funds has eroded at an astounding pace with no end in sight. The poverty level has reached the lowest levels in history. There are more people in the United States on food stamps than ever in the history of America. There are 20,000,000 illegals draining our economy. The national debt has increased to $13.4 trillion. Just how can the mainstream media report that the recession ended in June 2009? We would like to know what they are smoking.

GOD BLESS AMERICA

MY AMERICAN DREAM

Newsletter
Volume 2010-1   www.my-american-dream.org

This will be our first issue of the newsletter. We will strive to provide information that will not be covered in the mainstream media. We will attempt to be objective and fair in our newsletters and provide insight into some of the important things that are happening in the United States of America.

We hope to provide the American people with topics that are needed to consider in the course of rebuilding America to what the majority of the Americans truly desire!!

We feel that God should be part of everyone's lives and that any American can prey anytime that they desire. There should not be any separation of God from the United States. All of our money makes this statement. Look at every dollar bill. It will contain "In God We Trust". Why are so many people against prayers in our school system? This just does not make any sense.

It is very irritating that the President of the United States has abolished the National Prayer Day and then celebrates the Muslim Holy days. This is a major embarrassment and insult to the vast majority of the citizens. We need to reestablish our rights.

In our newsletters we are going to present our ideas with regard to the economy, unemployment, border security, immigration, taxes, bail outs, states rights, stimulus programs, credibility of the government, quality of our elected officials, lack of transparency, legislation crammed down our throats while the majority of the citizens are against it, racism and many other topics. We know that we will offend many people but that is alright. We are only trying to get the voting citizens to take a look at all sides of any proposal. If you are offended, then do not read the material and continue to vote blindly basing your opinions on the slanted major mainstream news media reports. Had you done some research in 2008 the United States would not be in the major mess it is today.

We want to contribute to making the United States the most respected and stable country in the world. We were there once and we need to do the things that take us back to that stature. Quit sucking up to other countries and be the leader of the world as we once were.

GOD BLESS AMERICA

CHAPTER TWENTY THREE

Proud to be an American

"PRIDE IN AMERICA"

I'm proud to be an American
I'm proud of the "Pledge of Allegiance"
I'm proud of the "National Anthem"
I'm proud to display the "American Flag"
I'm proud to defend the "American Freedoms"
I'm proud to communicate in "English"
I'm proud of freedom of "Religion"
I'm proud to be an American
God Bless the United States of America

Thomas R. Meinders

THE FINAL INSPECTION

The Soldier stood and faced God,
Which must always come to pass.
He hoped his shoes were shining,
Just as brightly as his brass..
'Step forward now, Soldier,

How shall I deal with you?
Have you always turned the other cheek?
To My Church have you been true?'
The soldier squared his shoulders and said,
'No, Lord, I guess I ain't.
Because those of us who carry guns,
Can't always be a saint.
I've had to work most Sundays,
And at times my talk was tough.
And sometimes I've been violent,
Because the world is awfully rough.
But, I never took a penny,
That wasn't mine to keep...
Though I worked a lot of overtime,
When the bills got just too steep.
And I never passed a cry for help,
Though at times I shook with fear..
And sometimes, God, forgive me,
I've wept unmanly tears.
I know I don't deserve a place,
Among the people here.
They never wanted me around,
Except to calm their fears
If you've a place for me here, Lord,
It needn't be so grand.
I never expected or had too much,
But if you don't, I'll understand.
There was a silence all around the throne,
Where the saints had often trod.
As the Soldier waited quietly,
For the judgment of his God.
'Step forward now, you Soldier,
You've borne your burdens well.
Walk peacefully on Heaven's streets,
You've done your time in Hell.'

Author Unknown~

It's the Soldier, not the reporter
Who has given us the freedom of the press.
It's the Soldier, not the poet,
Who has given us the freedom of speech.
It's the Soldier, not the politicians
That ensures our right to Life, Liberty and the Pursuit of Happiness.
It's the Soldier who salutes the flag,
Who serves beneath the flag,
And whose coffin is draped by the flag.

If you care to offer the smallest token of recognition
and appreciation for the Military,
Please pass this on and pray for our men and women
Who have served and are currently serving our country
And pray for those who have given the
ultimate sacrifice for freedom....

THESE COLORS DON'T RUN
AMEN

ABOUT THE AUTHOR

 I was born in Grundy Center, Iowa on October 21, 1937 and raised in Cedar Falls, Iowa until I enlisted in the United States Air Force. I have served my country for 8 years, 4 months and 6 days and have two honorable discharges to show for it. I am currently raising my 9 year old son as a single parent and living on social security. I have been in the stock brokerage business for about 20 years and an accountant for about 25 years. During the last 10 years I have attempted to help start-up companies to have a method of raising capital. As with all start-up companies some of them made it and the majority of them did not. That is just the nature of the start-up business. Through it all I have kept my sanity and have not lost my ability to think. I have been blessed with reasonable intelligence and have the ability to use common sense. I have also written "America Can Recover" "Bashing Sarah Palin" and "A Beautiful America"